Moment by Moment
Living with a Hole in my Heart

by Sharlene Campbell-Skinner

Manifest  Publishing

Copyright © 2016 by Sharlene Campbell Skinner

All content is copyright 2016 by Sharlene Campbell Skinner

All rights reserved worldwide.

No part of this book may be reproduced, redistributed, transmitted, retransmitted, translated, sold, given away, decompiled or otherwise circumvented by any means, electronic or mechanical, including photocopying, recording, or by any information storage or retrieval system, without written permission from the publisher, Manifest Publishing.

This book is designed to provide information and processes used by Sharlene Skinner. Every effort has been made to make it as complete and accurate as possible, but no warranty is implied.

The information in this book is provided on an "as is" basis. Manifesting Prosperity International, LLC, and the author make no guarantees that you will experience the same results as the author. The author and Manifesting Prosperity International, LLC also have no responsibility to any person or entity with respect to loss or damage arising from information contained in this book or from any programs or document that may accompany it.

ISBN-13: 978-1944913069
ISBN-10: 1944913068

Praise for Terrence

(Written in his Memory Book at his funeral.)

"ALL OF YOU CAN BE SO VERY PROUD OF TERRENCE. HE WAS SO PERCEPTIVE AND CONSIDERATE - ONE OF THE SINCEREST, WELL MANNERED GUYS WE KNOW. WE WELL REMEMBER TERRENCE WORKING FOR US YEARS AGO DOING YARD WORK AND STACKING WOOD. HE WAS ALWAYS A PLEASURE TO SPEAK WITH AND ALWAYS WILLING."

Kevin & Rose McVeigh
(Landlord for 10 years, Terrence worked for them)

"I HAVE FOND MEMORIES OF TERRENCE SINGING WITH THE FAMILY BIBLE WORSHIP TEAM. I ESPECIALLY REMEMBER HIM SINGING THE SONG, *YOU ARE SO GOOD TO ME*. IT REALLY TOUCHED MY HEART TO WHERE IT'S ONE OF MY MOST SPECIAL MEMORIES OF FAMILY BIBLE."

Judy Stevens
(Attended church with Terrence/Skinner's)

"MY MEMORIES OF TERRENCE ARE MANY. I WILL ALWAYS REMEMBER SOFTBALL WITH YOU & THE FAMILY BIBLE GROUP. YOU STEPPED UP AS OUR COACH AND ROOTED US ALL ON. THOSE WERE THE BEST SUMMERS OF MY LIFE. WORSHIP PRACTICES WERE GREAT, TOO. WE HAD A LOT OF FUN GOOFING OFF AND

LAUGHING. AND, I ALWAYS KNEW YOUR HEART FOR MUSIC & YOUR LOVE FOR LYNDSAY. YOU WILL BE GREATLY MISSED, TERRENCE. AND THIS SUMMER, WE PLAY BALL FOR YOU!

YOU HAVE LEFT A FINGERPRINT ON MY LIFE, TERRENCE.

CHRIS SAYS HE MISSES YOU, AND HE LOVES YOU & YOUR FAMILY. HE SAID YOU WERE A GREAT MAN."

Carrie Magee
*(Team ma*te on softball *team* and on *worship team)*

"YOU WILL BE GREATLY MISSED. I CAN'T COUNT HOW MANY TIMES YOU WOULD COME TO OUR HOUSE TO HANG OUT WITH DANIEL, BUT YOU WOULD END UP PLAYING ON THE FLOOR FOR HOURS WITH ZACH, LETTING HIM JUST CLIMB ALL OVER YOU. NOT ONLY WERE YOU OUR FRIEND, YOU WERE ZACH'S, TOO. I'M SO GLAD TO HAVE BEEN A PART OF YOUR LIFE, AND THAT YOU WERE ABLE TO MEET LIZZIE. THOSE FIRE PIT NIGHTS AT BEV AND MARTY'S HOUSE WILL NEVER BE THE SAME WITHOUT YOU THERE."

Daniel, Jessica, Zach & Lizzie
(Friends of Terrence's, Daniel was a pallbearer)

"Terrence was always a positive, respectful person that everyone loved. We all went to prom and met at prom together. He was always making jokes and smiling."

Rebekah Burrell
(Classmate)

"Terrence always had a smile on his face. He was a sweet friend to have and was always there for you. I remember in sixth grade going on field trips, especially to The Stern Wheeler. Great Times! We all love & will miss Terrence tons! He's in everyone's thoughts and memories."

Rachael (Speers) Travis
(Classmate)

"It's so hard to pick just one memory, although little league is probably the most memorable. Terrence was always the team's morale booster. He always tried to make the best of everything & bring out the best in all of those around him.

He truly was a special person, and will always have a place in my heart."

Andrew David Mier
(Classmate)

"I was nervous about attending our 10-year reunion. I wasn't exactly a nice person back then, but I'm glad I went. The minute Terrence arrived, he gave me a huge hug and told me how great it was to see me. Terrence was the type of guy who everyone loved, you just couldn't help yourself. I will miss him every year at Civil War (OSU vs UO) time, we teased each other mercilessly because we were football rivals. Terrence touched my life in so many ways and I will sorely miss him."

Luanne Johnson
(Classmate)

"It was such a privilege to have our children grow up together. Meggy couldn't have had two finer friends than Terrence and Chase (Terrence's brother.) With the love of children who have special needs, it was such a blessing to know Terrence had a special place in his heart for kids faced with adversity and differences."

Sandy Marchbanks
(Family Friend)

"Words to describe Terrence:

- ✝ Love
- ✝ Respectful
- ✝ Joy
- ✝ A Lover of Jesus
- ✝ Fun
- ✝ Laughter
- ✝ A "Big Duck"
  (Terrence loved the Oregon Ducks)
- ✝ A friend
- ✝ A son
- ✝ A treasure
- ✝ One who will be missed!"

Debie Wyne
(Family Friend)

"Terrence was special!! He was such a great friend to my boys, all three. Brandon and Daniel's, best friend like a brother. To Adam, he was the big guy who always played with him at the ball games from the time he was three until even now, playing Halo and having a great time together. We loved Terrence like our own. Fire nights on the patio won't be he same. We love you Terrence and you are already missed."

Beverly Leoopard
(Family Friend, another mama to Terrence)

"One of my favorite things Terrence did, was to talk like Bob Dylan. He was very good at it. I made me laugh every time I heard him. Terrence always had a smile on his face and a hug for you. Terrence was a good friend. I worked with Terrence at Growing Oaks."

Jackie
(Co-worker at Growing Oaks Daycare Center)

"I was most impressed at Chase's wedding when the Best Man, Terrence, testified of an amazing friendship that he and his brother had. It is hard to put into words what I saw that day. What Terrence said so impacted me."

Bob Ruddiman
(Family Friend)

"One of my memories of Terrence was when he left his job at Growing Oaks to work at the Children's Home/Farm Home School, where he was at his time of death. He wrote a letter to all the parents about why he was leaving. I was so impressed with his letter. I was sad to see him leave, but his letter talked about his love for kids and wanting to work with kids who he could really help. It said a lot to me as to his character. He will be missed."

Deana Grobe
(Growing Oaks Parent)

(The following is a portion of an email from the lady who was Terrence's boss at the time of his death. Email was received Fall of 2009 after Terrence died.)

"WE STILL THINK OF TERRENCE AND REFER TO HIM OFTEN. TERRENCE WAS MY 'MASCOT' AS I CALLED HIM. IN OTHER WORDS, HE WAS THE PERSON I DEPENDED ON TO CONTINUE THE POSITIVE, GOOD ATTITUDE AMONG STAFF. BECAUSE OF HIS WORK, WE CREATED A SUPPORTIVE, HAPPY, POSITIVE WORKING CULTURE AMONG ALL STAFF. THEY ALL LOVE IT HERE. SO, I THANK TERRENCE DAILY, FROM MY HEART."

Judy McCormick

In Memory

My son, Terrence, you showed me
how to live like Jesus in everyday life.
I love you, Terr, and I miss you.

Acknowledgements

I want to thank Lee, my husband, for seeing and believing in me and this book. He has always been the first to provide, protect, love and encourage me in my every day life, as well as any new adventure or endeavor I have taken. He has walked with me in the darkest time of my life, and I am so thankful for the commitment we made November 4, 1978 to love, honor and cherish until death do us part. He is one of the kindest, gentlest, most loving souls I have ever known, and I am thankful daily for him.

I want to thank my son, Chase. He has loved me and helped me laugh when I was sure I could never laugh again. Each day I thank God for Chase, seeing him grow and develop into the man of God he has become. He has an amazing wife, Stephanie, who is an ideal mate and fits into our family perfectly. Since the beginning of this project, we've been blessed to add Raegan Marie Skinner to our family. She is Chase and Stephanie's daughter, our first granddaughter. We are so thankful for Raegan, the blessing she is to Chase and Stephanie, the growing of their family, which grows our family. Our cup runneth over.

I am thankful for Terrence's wife (at the time of his death), Lyndsay, who has shown me in ways she doesn't even realize, how to draw from my faith and move forward with strength and courage. I am moved to tears by Lyndsay's sheer will to find her "new normal" in life, seeking God as she goes. She was a blessing to Terrence, and she is a blessing to me.

I want to thank everyone who offered to read, review, edit and just love me through the process, you are angels in human form. I am so grateful to my sister, Sherry, who surprised me with two copies of my book for my 55th birthday. It was the catalyst that pushed me to contact a publisher and move forward with getting my book published.

Thank you to my father and mother-in-law, Warren and Carole Skinner, who have never said no to me, when I have asked for their support in any form, and they helped me financially get my dream into print. They have taught me such generosity and what it means to give without asking anything in return.

There are no words to convey in any manner that adequately honors my family and friends and all who loved our Terrence, and me. To each of you who have shown me Jesus with a message, text, card, phone call, or visit to our home—thank you.

We have the blessing of family functions which bring us together and so many we are loved by and whom we dearly love. I am truly thankful for each opportunity to be with those precious to me, whether family, friend, or casual contact. Jesus loves his "kids," and so do I.

To a women's gathering that helped me identify and work through areas of my life that needed attention in the continuation of my "Kingdom work" that is before me, God in his wisdom knew this was a "season" of dealing and healing just for me. I believe he provided the gathering venue for this to happen. Bless each of you who ministered to me through those weeks and loved me with the unconditional love of Jesus.

I want to thank you, Lord Jesus, for gently preparing me for this project, even in the midst of the shattering numbness when I didn't know if I could take another breath. I am a living testimony to the Lord's promises in the darkest time of my life.

"THE LORD IS CLOSE TO THE BROKENHEARTED AND SAVES THOSE WHO ARE CRUSHED IN SPIRIT." PSALM 34:18 (NIV)

Table of Contents

CHAPTER 1 GOD IS GOOD ALL THE TIME 1

CHAPTER 2 HE IS TRUTH 15

CHAPTER 3 HE LOVES US 27

CHAPTER 4 DEATH IS UGLY 39

CHAPTER 5 ETERNITY IS REAL 61

CHAPTER 6 CRAZY THINGS PEOPLE SAY 77

CHAPTER 7 WE GET TO GO 85

CHAPTER 8 LIFE HAPPENS 97

CHAPTER 9 NO REGRETS 105

CHAPTER 10 MORE THAN SURVIVORS 119

Moment by Moment
Living with a Hole in my Heart

The Broken Chain

We little knew that morning,
that God was going to call your name
In life we loved you dearly,
in death we do the same.

It broke our hearts to lose you,
You did not go alone;
For part of us went with you
The day God called you home.

You left us peaceful memories,
Your life is still our guide;
And though we cannot see you,
You are always at our side.

Our family chain is broken,
And nothing seems the same;
But as God calls us one by one,
The chain will link again.

Ron Tranmer

Preface

It feels betraying for me to write that I praise God daily for taking our son Terrence only days before Christmas in 2008. He died very quickly of sepsis. In the days that have come and gone since we had to let go of Terrence in this physical realm, I have come to realize that it is only through Terrence's death that I am finding the "truths" that I base my life on.

These are many of the same truths that Terrence based his upon as well.

The Lord encouraged me within hours of my son's passing that I should journal my journey. Writing in a form other than expressing my grieving, my raw feelings, came later. I knew even before we left the hospital after Terrence's death, that our lives would never be the same. I wondered, "How am I going to do this?"

My husband, Lee, constantly encouraged me along the way as I began to write out my feelings. It was Lee who encouraged me to take up my keyboard and begin. Lee, Terrence, and my second son, Chase, have always been my cheerleaders; championing on my behalf whatever thoughts or endeavors I was pursuing, yet somehow feeling uncertain.

A Poem written on October 11, 2009
at Pine Grove Cemetery

Death has claimed your life as we knew it here,
Heaven has you, so we wait with no fear,
Until the Lord calls us home, our place with him won
Seeing you again, our sweet earthly son.

To spend eternity worshipping and praising the risen God
No more pain, fear or brokenness of this Earth we trod
Only joy and happiness await us each
When our journey as we know it here will be done.

Family, friends, and all the saints
Who already have gone ahead
We will all sit at the banqueting table
With the King and be fed.
Only peace and love will be my forever reward
For a life I have chosen to declare and serve my Lord.

Daily seeking his face, his path to not miss
Knowing someday behind me, I'll leave all of this.
So until the angels come,
My "graduation" party, my turn to go home,
I will continue to praise God; his son to call my own.

I will miss you every day, Terrence,
And can hardly wait until I see you again.

"For I know the plans I have for you," declares the Lord, Plans to prosper you and not to harm you, Plans to give you hope and a future."

Jeremiah 29:11 (NIV)

"Mourning is not disbelieving. Flooded eyes don't represent a faithless heart. A person can enter a cemetery Jesus-certain of life after death and still have a Twin Tower crater in the heart. Christ did. Grief does not mean you don't trust; it simply means you can't stand the thought of another day without the Lazarus of your life."

Max Lucado

"I thought of you with love today but that is nothing new. I thought about you yesterday and days before that too. I think of you in silence and often speak your name All I have are memories and your picture in a frame. Your memory is my keepsake with which I never part; God has you in his keeping, I have you in my heart."

Anonymous

Chapter 1
God Is Good All the Time

"FOR THE LORD IS GOOD AND HIS LOVE ENDURES FOREVER; HIS FAITHFULNESS CONTINUES THROUGH ALL GENERATIONS." PSALM 100:5 (NIV)

None of us know when we will be in a situation that will change everything we have been taught, everything we have believed, and everything we have trusted. We, as a family faced that encounter on December 20, 2008. Our sweet firstborn son, Terrence Glenn Skinner, husband, son, and brother, went to Jesus that morning after less than 24 hours in Critical Care at the Albany Oregon Hospital. He was only 29 years old.

I want you each to know the loves of my life: Jesus, Lee (my husband of 37 years), sons Terrence and Chase. I have never been so blessed at any time in my life as I am in the role of wife and mother. I adore my husband, and I love my kids beyond measure. My family is the perfect example of "God is good all the time."

My husband and I directed junior high and high school camps for years. The one thing we always taught the kids was, "God is good all the time. All the time God is good." We had the privilege of being a part of something so real and so perfect, in a Kingdom realm, this side of Heaven. We loved the opportunity to do camp every year and this was our "family vacation" each year.

Rarely did we go or do what would be considered the normal family vacation. I believe I can speak for the four of us saying we truly looked forward to camp every year. We loved those days of "Jesus shows up," healing, loving and showing us His plans and His glory. Those were amazing summers we will never forget, and we now treasure in our hearts.

Lee and I married on November 4, 1978, and Terrence was conceived in December of 1978. We wasted no time. Terrence was God's gift to us, and we knew as soon as he was born, he was going to be very special in the Kingdom. Before I met Lee, he had an encounter with the Lord, who told him clearly, "Your firstborn will serve me." What a promise before we were even blessed with Terrence! And yes, he did serve the Lord. He loved and showed Jesus to a lost world in his everyday life. I pray that I can show Jesus just like Terrence did.

It was April 1982 that we were blessed again with Chase, another perfect example of God's goodness. Chase loved his big brother, and Terrence adored his little brother. We could hardly keep Terrence from hugging and kissing on Chase when we brought him home from the hospital.

Terrence loved sports even at an early age.

This was just the beginning of an amazing 'earthly' bond that would form between two brothers. Our sons were blessed with the sweetest, most kind, compassionate spirits and the most amazing senses of humor. Many times I have said, "What a gift that we spent so much time with our kids and the hours of laughter we have had."

We have a neighbor who told my husband one time that, "He always wondered what we were laughing about always having so much fun on our deck." That's just what we do. We loved spending time together, talking, living, loving and laughing. I never knew that those days would be limited with Terrence, but I know he is alive and happier than he has ever been.

I have come to know firsthand what is meant by the scripture,

"EVEN IN LAUGHTER THE HEART MAY ACHE AND JOY MAY END IN GRIEF." PROVERBS 14:13 (NIV)

The good news, I should say the "God" news is, we are laughing more, and joy is being restored. We are finding our new "normal," and it's OK!

Within three years of marrying, I had gotten my two sons, and I had my dear husband. I had much to testify to the goodness of God at a very early place in my marriage. It took me some years and seeing things through the eyes of the Father to come to a greater understanding of the blessed life I have.

Lee and I spent the first eight years of marriage on a farm in South Dakota. It was farming, struggling, and raising our boys. I worked at various jobs in our local town. Things were stressful, as they were for all farmers in the 80's, and eventually we left the farm.

We moved to another town not far from there and worked there for almost three years. Life began to move the valve atop our pressure cooker more than any other time in our marriage. We were working different shifts, not in the best environment, struggling financially, and not serving God. We both always had "knowledge" of who the Lord was, and we both had plenty of "religion." What we were missing was "relationship." I believe there was a defining moment in our marriage, and Lee was the one who prayed, "Lord, whatever it takes, I give her to you."

We had discussed moving somewhere and had no idea where that might be. Not long after Lee prayed, I would venture to say within days, I was in agreement for a change. We decided to put our mobile home and lots up for sale. We made homemade signs and a flyer for placement in the local Laundromat. We were selling our home and moving.

We were told there were trailers and stick homes for sale for years and that we would never sell ours. Granted, this was from someone who was not encouraging in our lives and who didn't know Jesus.

Within 24 hours we had a couple who wanted to buy our home.

"God is good all the time" even when we don't see it. The Lord was working to fulfill *His* plan for our lives, not our plan for our lives. Even if we thought at the time it was us who had it all worked out.

We knew our boys were at an age that if we were going to move, it needed to be soon; before they were too old and really attached to school and friends. Now by no means was it easy moving them or us, but there was "something" drawing us to Oregon.

I spoke to my older sister who was encouraging and offered us their home as a temporary home when we got to Oregon. So that was "our" plan. Lee's parents, two of the most amazing people I have ever known, moved us there. Our earthly belongings were packed in the back of their pickup truck, and we were westward bound. It was a very emotional move, but once again, there was a "pull" we both felt, and a "peace" we had never known before.

"BECAUSE OF THE TENDER MERCY OF OUR GOD, BY WHICH THE RISING SUN WILL COME TO US FROM HEAVEN. TO SHINE ON THOSE LIVING IN DARKNESS AND IN THE SHADOW OF DEATH, TO GUIDE OUR FEET INTO THE PATH OF PEACE." LUKE 1:78-79 (NIV)

We are so deeply loved by the Father that He was guiding our feet in peace and leading us to what His plan was for us. That was the summer of 1987.

We moved to Oregon, lived with my sister for a time, and made our new home in the beautiful Willamette Valley, where to this day we remain. The boys adapted well, were fun loving, easy going, loved by their friends and thoroughly enjoyed life.

After Terrence went to Jesus and since, I have spent hours looking at pictures and missing my sweet little boy. He was a happy baby, little boy, young man, and man of God. There was joy and happiness that surrounded Terrence even as a baby.

In later years, Terrence had struggles and heartaches (like all of us), but God had His "fingerprints" all over Terrence from day one. He was marked for great things.

"IF YOU BELONGED TO THE WORLD, IT WOULD LOVE YOU AS ITS OWN. AS IT IS, YOU DO NOT BELONG TO THE WORLD, BUT I HAVE CHOSEN YOU OUT OF THE WORLD." JOHN 15:19 (NIV)

It was clear that Terrence was chosen out of the world. It just took Terrence some time to find his way to the heart of the Father and "His" will. I praise God daily that Terrence made the choice to have Jesus as his personal savior, and now Terrence is in the presence of God. We will be together again; no more tears or "See ya soon." I try not to say goodbye to the ones I love. I say, "See ya soon."

"Do not let your hearts be troubled. Trust in God; trust also in me. In my Father's house are many rooms; if it were not so, I would have told you. I am going there to prepare a place for you. And if I go and prepare a place for you, I will come back and take you to be with me that you also may be where I am." John 14: 1-3 (NIV)

I had a dear friend, Jean Johnson, who went to be with the Lord in July, right before Terrence. She loved the passage in John that told of the mansion that was being built, just for her. She would have it read to her as she waited for her "graduation party" into Heaven. I miss you, too, sweet friend.

God in all His goodness had prepared a place for Terrence, a party was waiting like none we will ever experience on Earth, and Terrence got to go on the morning of December 20, 2008. I am struck with such awe at my sweet Terrence in the presence of God, angels, ancients of old, friends, family, loved ones, it is overwhelming. God in His goodness and mercy took Terrence home swiftly, I believe sparing us from any long suffering here.

As I continue to walk this side of Heaven without my sweet son, I am made so keenly aware of how fleeting all of "this" is, but that there is also a purpose and plan that is only attainable by me. A message and ministry that can only be done by me and it is so tightly woven to the death of my son.

Now, there are so many things I would rather pick or do in this life than to be in this, "Mothers who have lost a child" club. The reality is that this is a unique club. A cousin of mine who lost her daughter months after I lost Terrence, replied to a post I had made on Facebook, and she was the one who actually mentioned the club we were are now a part of, not by our choosing!

In the same year Terrence died, I lost my best friend. We also said goodbye to a dearly loved neighbor, a great friend to both Lee and I, and then we lost Terrence. We have seen so much death in our 35 years of marriage, but I can tell you that we have never seen so much Hope in the midst of such tragedy either.

I, as a mother, have never been able to understand how anyone who loses a child could continue living if they didn't have the assurance their child was with Jesus. For Lee and me, we are so blessed and thankful for the choices Terrence made along the way that led him to the throne room of God. I am also eternally grateful for every friend, family member and loved one we have lost to death, for their profound choice to serve a Living God. There is the promise and hope of seeing them again and spending eternity with them. Thank you, Jesus, for your sacrifice.

It goes without saying that as I continue to walk this life, there is so much that I in my own flesh would change, but God in all his wisdom and whom I trust, is far better equipped to guide my life.

Terrence was our cheerleader. He was such a good and perfect gift, straight from the heart of God. Lee and I know that we had a very special and unique son, with a huge heart, who accepted without judgment, and who showed Jesus daily to a dying world. He was probably the purest earthly example of Jesus that I personally have ever been witness to.

Terrence was the kind of person that after you met him, he drew you into his world and you wanted to be his friend. He took time to listen, to really listen, to people. Many people have shared with me since Terrence's death, that when they had a problem or needed someone to talk to, Terrence was the one who would listen for hours. He had a very soft spirit and the kindest heart I have ever known.

There is irony, however sad, in the fact that his last organ to be attacked by sepsis (a disease of the blood) was his sweet, kind heart!

Terrence had undiagnosed diabetes.

His count, if I remember correctly, was 1400-ish when he was in ER. He had not been sick at any length. He came home Thursday afternoon not feeling good, and by Friday morning was in an irreversible coma. He was taken to ER Friday morning, then to Critical Unit, where we spent the next 20 hours crying out for a miracle. It was decided that Terrence had sepsis (which is usually fatal) and that he probably had an internal injury that it attacked. Then the sepsis spread through his blood, killing major organs as it went.

His internal doctor believed Terrence probably had appendicitis. He was too sick for the doctors to try anything exploratory and an autopsy was out of the question. I also know that the information that would have been gathered, would have benefitted the "medical community," but would not change what was happening in Kingdom realm. Terrence was with

Jesus, and we were without Terrence…and five days to Christmas.

We spent Christmas Eve 2008 at the funeral home. I have never felt so sad, empty, lost or broken in my life. Once again, Terrence was never more alive, that is what was truly going on in Kingdom. The next days were a blur, details, planning, casket, flowers, and memorial service. God in all His goodness, I believe without a doubt, took our Terrence quickly; sparing us prolonged suffering here and even more importantly, spared Terrence that suffering.

As we waited, believing, crying out and praying, I did not at that point in the hospital foresee Terrence not being with us, not leaving the hospital alive. God in His wisdom and goodness knew what was best, and I never doubted that Terrence was with God. And, I was never more aware that he would never be with us again, here on this side of forever.

I have to share that "Terrence" means "tender-hearted and gently formed." There are not words that more accurately describe him. He was a true gift to us and a living example of God's goodness and blessing in our lives. I am a very grateful mother who will forever thank God for picking me to be Terrence's mom and for giving me the years I had Terrence with me. My flesh and heart know they were not enough, but everything I believe and know of Kingdom tells me there was no mistake made in Terrence's "going home" to his Heavenly home. I am daily and often moment by moment finding a way to live with the "Terr" hole in my heart.

Some days breathing is easier than others, and some days I'm not sure I want to go on breathing! The pain stays; some days it pierces and hurts more, and other days it is a dull ache. Some days, I even get through hours without thinking of Terrence. I know all that I feel is normal for the grieving process.

I will tell you from my own personal experience that "time does not heal." Time passes and you make choices, daily choices to live, love and embrace what you have today. It is an everyday choice when I open my eyes and hear my heart beating, to choose who I will serve this day.

I know that no matter how "lost" I feel in everyday life, that Terrence has never been more "found." All he heard, thought, read, was taught, dreamed or hoped for beyond this life was revealed in clarity and glory when he exhaled his last breath. Terrence became part of an eternal community, his "forever" home.

I heard a speaker sharing how longing for "forever" was God's idea and placed deep within our spirit. I found such comfort in hearing that. I have thought many times since Terrence died that there was something wrong with me, or I wasn't in my right frame of mind at times. There is a longing that I feel for "home," a home that is unlike any I have known. I find myself longing, groaning, crying for "forever" and feel guilty that I am not thankful or taking full advantage of everything I have been blessed with in this life.

So, it was a tremendous comfort and relief to hear someone share how it is completely natural and a God buried desire in every one of us. Thank you, Father, for placing such a natural desire in my heart to long to be with you and all that I have loved and lost.

"MEANWHILE WE GROAN, LONGING TO BE CLOTHED WITHOUT HEAVENLY DWELLING." 2 CORINTHIANS 5:2

My family: Terrence, Lee, me and Chase at Chase and Stephanie's wedding. One day we'll be reunited...FOREVER.

Chapter 2
He Is Truth

"Guide me in your truth and teach me, for you are God, my Savior, and my hope is in you all day long." Psalm 25:5 (NIV)

Terrence would say to me, "Keep it real, Mom. Keep it real."

What I believe he was saying and not even aware of maybe, was "Speak truth." Every day we find ourselves in situations that challenge the very core of what we believe. In those days to day moments, we have a choice that impacts and changes our lives in ways we have no way of knowing at the moment. The important thing is to "choose right; choose truth; choose justice; choose love."

Terrence's life was never easy. There were seasons in his life where he seemed to turn left when it was clearly right, and he chose up when the obvious was down.

Terrence and Lyndsay were married for almost

two and a half years. Years that were packed with more love and joy than many of us will see in our lifetime. There was a restoration that they brought to each other's lives. It was a divine plan of the Father heart of God.

Terrence and Lyndsay worked in the same place when they met. Terrence had many "friends" that were female, but he was looking for love. Terrence did not waste time in his relationship with Lyndsay. I remember him telling me that he had talked with Lyndsay. He had shared with her that, "He was not in their relationship to pass time; he was serious." I think that moved things right along, needless to say. It was obvious that they truly loved each other and God was at work.

Lyndsay shares that when she met Terrence she thought, "He was a Bible thumper." Terrence would say that when he met Lyndsay, "She was buck wild." This came to be quite a joke and many laughs were shared at their first opinions of each other. Although, perceived as a "Bible thumper," there was something different about Terrence that Lyndsay was drawn to. I knew what "it" was and soon Lyndsay would, too.

Terrence made it known that he loved the Lord and this was his life. Lyndsay understood religion, but would come to see firsthand what a relationship with Jesus was like. They were growing by leaps and bounds, which we were blessed to see the man and woman of God that they were becoming; knit together by their love for each other and for Jesus.

There was a naturalness to the Jesus who Terrence showed to the world in his day to day living. He probably didn't even realize it, as it came with such ease. Oh, he was human and had his days and "flesh flashes" like we all do, but at the core of who he was and who he loved (and wanted to model his life after) was Jesus. He had a core desire to honor and serve.

We all are born with a God hole inside of us. Many of us will pack it full of the world. Terrence did this, too, in certain seasons of his searching. But deep down, he knew what was true and lasting. He went through various relationships that took a part of his heart, left him broken, and seeking…praise God for Lyndsay and the restoration that would come from her love and patience with Terrence.

"And the God of all grace, who called you to His eternal glory in Christ, after you have suffered a little while, will himself restore you and make you strong, firm, and steadfast."
I Peter 5:10 (NIV)

Terrence went through a program at a local town close to us. It was a "restoration" program, and it changed his life forever, literally. They were leaders, brothers and sisters in Christ, who loved Terrence through an unbelievably broken time in his life. I am grateful for every lesson, every prayer, every person who was involved with this program—it anchored Terrence in Jesus anew. He was apprehensive and did not want to go, but his mother (me) who loved him beyond words, strongly encouraged him to go. He shared some time later that he was so grateful for my "persistence" and those who loved him through restoration.

There was truth taught and guidance was given in Godly, biblical principles that set the stage for a second chance for Terrence in love. True revelations of the "Father's heart" for Terrence were being made known. Healing from his past and preparation for future were instrumental in the road that led Terrence to the throne room of God. Through the years we would sit and reminisce of God's faithfulness and plans that were concretely grounded in Terrence's weekly choices (restoration) to be broken and poured out, so the new could come in.

"AND NO ONE POURS NEW WINE INTO OLD WINESKINS."
LUKE 5:37 (NIV)

Terrence was being readied for the new wine. The old wineskin was going. Restoration was a painful process that found my sweet son in tears every day for some time. He was going through this without very many people even realizing his suffering. He desired to be changed from the inside out. God was faithful to hear his cries and showed him mercy.

"OUT OF THE DEPTHS I CRY TO YOU, O LORD. O LORD, HEAR MY VOICE. LET YOUR EARS BE ATTENTIVE TO MY CRY FOR MERCY." PSALM 129:1- 2 (NIV)

We all go through seasons. Some of us go through

years of looking for truth. Many have given in to false or fake truths that left us more broken and damaged than before we began. It is one of the most amazing transformations that can happen to a living person, the revelation of the one true living God and His unconditional love for us. He is just waiting for us to accept all that is freely ours.

"AND WE ARE JUSTIFIED FREELY BY HIS GRACE AND THROUGH THE REDEMPTION THAT CAME BY CHRIST JESUS." ROMANS 3:24(NIV)

What an awe-striking thought to know that His word tells us that we are justified freely, by His grace and redeeming power. The times we live in do not offer too much freely. There is usually quite a price to be paid. The living God of the universe has freely paid by His son's death the price for us. None of us is deserving of this gift; each of us has sinned. Yet he chose and knew that by the sacrifice that would be made by his very own son, we would be made free. This is such a wondrous knowledge in truth and freedom being so closely woven by grace.

I want to reference back to the very first pages and chapter of this book where I had mentioned the promise God had given Lee. God is true to His word and His promises. He always will fulfill what He has said. The Lord had given Lee the promise, almost 30 years before Terrence's death, that His firstborn would serve Him. That is the sovereign will of the Father and those plans that were set in eternal realms did come to pass.

Give God praise for every good and perfect gift you have in your life. I don't mean the house, the car, the job, but every good and perfect gift. I have always said, "I spend time with my eyes to the sky, looking for the fireworks that light the entire sky. While God is more concerned that I don't miss the little sparkler that will change me forever." Once again, I praise God for the fizzlers and the sparklers; they are changing me and taking me from glory to glory.

It has taken me years and immeasurable grief to understand that I will not see the "miracle" I am petitioning, weeping (and even begging for sometimes) this side of Heaven. That truth is, the miracle happened, just not how I wanted it to. God doesn't always say, "Yes." Believe me, I know that first hand, and he doesn't always say, "No," either.

I have struggled with being told, "God is doing or allowing what is best for me." I have had to step away from profound loss and grief. Cling to every truth that I have ever been told or read. I ask often, "Lord how can losing Terrence be good for me?" I know the many answers to this question before I ask, but I still ask.

Lee and I both know that we would not be who we are today were it not for the gracious love of a

Heavenly Father who took Terrence to his "forever" home.

Do we like Terrence not being with us? No!

Yet, we know that everything of Kingdom and spirit that bears witness with us tells us, Terrence is in his Father's house. The struggle we have is with our minds, flesh and heart. At battle with each other and sometimes pitted against everything, we know of truth. I have praised God (even before I left Terrence's Critical Care room) he was already in Heaven, for Terrence's choices that led him into the presence of God, forever!

We are learning to find our "new normal" in everyday living, to not dread the adjustments and changes that have come, to accept the things I have seen because God loves me so much and knows for this mom's heart, those things were necessary. I have never been alone, nor will I ever be.

"TRUST IN THE LORD WITH ALL YOUR HEART AND LEAN NOT ON YOUR OWN UNDERSTANDING. IN ALL YOUR WAYS ACKNOWLEDGE HIM AND HE WILL MAKE YOUR PATHS STRAIGHT." PROVERBS 3:5 (NIV)

I am, in ways that I never thought possible, finding out what it means to trust with all my heart and to acknowledge him in all my ways. I have always believed as a Christian, that I do a good job of trusting and acknowledging who God is, and who I am not. I have found out in the last few years since losing Terrence that I wasn't doing a very good job. I was not trusting or acknowledging with all my heart or mind. It is very convenient to allow God in, just as far as we think we feel we need Him to be in our lives. Wait until desperation sets in, and you don't know if you can even take another breath, let alone have any energy for any form of life or activity!

I am also being blessed by the God who loves me so desperately and without measure by his desire to "make my paths straight." You go through this life doing what you believe is right and good, not even realizing in the process, how crooked everything has gotten. There were very "crooked" places in my heart, when it came to the "truth" of the all that God wanted and wants from me.

We have all done a good job of smiling through the worst pain in our lives, masking, deadening, or ignoring the deep things of God that are just within our reach. Life deals us a bad hand, we reshuffle the cards all the time, but there is so much more within that deck. The "deuce" or "2" is one of the lowest cards in the deck. There is a card game where the "3" cannot be taken from you. It is a "promised" point to whoever holds the card. That is how Kingdom works, when we accept Jesus as our personal savior, it is a "promise" that no one can take from us. We can make choices that grieve the Father's heart, but He never changes. He never gives up on us. That is Kingdom truth.

"FOR GOD SO LOVED THE WORLD THAT HE GAVE HIS ONE AND ONLY SON, THAT WHOEVER BELIEVES IN HIM SHALL NOT PERISH BUT HAVE ETERNAL LIFE." JOHN 3:16 (NIV)

We all, from a young age, have heard, read, or been taught the above scripture. It is one of the most amazing promises and truths that can be found. When the days are long, the grief is deep, the crying will not cease, and I can hardly breathe, I am encouraged by the promise that He gave His ONLY Son for me. I, as a mother, am encouraged and hopeful at the thought that God gave his son for my son. I have had a comfort that goes beyond words and a hope to equal that I will see Terrence again. Many days, the really long days and nights, I long for Heaven and to be in the presence of the Lord. One of my favorite "visual" scriptures is in Revelation in the fourth chapter where it is describing the Throne in Heaven.

"HOLY, HOLY, HOLY IS THE LORD GOD ALMIGHTY, WHO WAS, AND IS, AND IS TO COME." REVELATION 4:8 (NIV)

This scripture is one of the "truths" that I cling to, longing for the day when I will be a part of a "holy" assembly around the throne of God. Terrence will be there, my dear friend Jean, brothers, dad and mom, and so many more who I long to see again.

Lights of my life, Chase and Terrence.

Chapter 3
He Loves Us

"AND SO WE KNOW AND RELY ON THE LOVE GOD HAS FOR US. GOD IS LOVE. WHOEVER LIVES IN LOVE, LIVES IN GOD AND GOD IN HIM. I JOHN 4:15 (NIV)

God's heart is to always have his children know how loved they are, how precious they are, and how he sent His son to die for them. Jesus' death on the cross was God's promise to us that we would have an eternal home with Him and how much He was willing to sacrifice for us.

Lee and I both went back to work about a week after Terrence's funeral. I knew that I had to keep my hands and mind busy. For me, I did not want to spin out to a place that I wasn't certain I could make it back from! I had more grace and flexibility allowed at my job than Lee did. We both have found even in the months and years that have passed, when we sit and think too long, that is when the loss and brokenness begins to close in so closely. It is hard to breathe. We continue to cry out to the one true God for strength, hope, grace, and endurance for the moment because many days are lived, moment to moment.

I praise God for the "routine" of our lives. It comes with subtlety, pulling me back into the ebb and flow of living. This, by far, was not something that happened instantly.

Terrence and Liana Bumstead Innskeep at High School Camp. They were both counselors. Terrence loved camp and did it for 10 years.

There were days I wondered if I would ever feel any form of "normal" again in my life. I can say without weeping or anger that we have, and have continued to live in our "new normal."

Many days (more than I am sure I know), I can see Terrence saying, "See Father, that's my mom and dad there." I try daily to enter the flow of this world with my life, in my little corner of the world, with conviction, hope and a love shown me by Terrence, but greater yet, by a Heavenly Father.

"FOR OUR LIGHT AND MOMENTARY TROUBLES ARE ACHIEVING FOR US AN ETERNAL GLORY THAT FAR OUTWEIGHS THEM ALL. SO WE FIX OUR EYES NOT ON WHAT IS SEEN, BUT ON WHAT IS UNSEEN. FOR WHAT IS SEEN IS TEMPORARY, BUT WHAT IS UNSEEN IT ETERNAL." II CORINTHIANS 4:17-18 (NIV)

A few days after we had gone back to work, I "hit the wall." I couldn't stop crying; breathing was difficult; and anything that should have brought comfort did not. As clearly as I hear my own heartbeat or music in the background, I heard the Father say so clearly, "I know this is almost unbearable and you are feeling so lost, but I promise it will all make sense someday." God clearly spoke to me, giving me His promise and with that promise I felt a calm and peace that I needed in that moment.

"PEACE I LEAVE WITH YOU; MY PEACE I GIVE YOU. I DO NOT GIVE TO YOU AS THE WORLD GIVES. DO NOT LET YOUR HEART BE TROUBLED AND DO NOT BE AFRAID." JOHN 14:27 (NIV)

The peace of God is so perfect and so real, it is tangible. It is felt; it wraps itself around you and gently whispers, "You're going to be OK." So much of my younger years were spent wanting to be OK, but there is nothing like growing in the love and knowledge of our Heavenly Father who gave His most precious gift for us! There is no greater act of love, in my opinion, that shows me how much I am loved than God sacrificing His "only" Son for me.

"FOR GOD SO LOVED THE WORLD THAT HE GAVE HIS ONE AND ONLY SON, THAT WHOEVER BELIEVES IN HIM SHALL NOT PERISH BUT HAVE ETERNAL LIFE." JOHN 3:16 (NIV)

I have been mindful so many times of the unbelievable unconditional love that God has for me. So much so, that I am usually moved to tears. I would have never would have thought in any of the years of raising my sons or seeing them grow into men of God, that there was any greater joy or gift. I was mistaken. There was the sacrifice that was made so long ago for me, my husband, my sons, for all of us.

From the moment the doctor walked out of Terrence's room and into the hall outside of Critical Care and told those of us waiting and pleading before the throne that, "Terrence is gone," and that, "We did all that we could," I was so acutely aware of God's son, taking the place of my son.

And, at that instant, Terrence was with God.

There is no greater peace for a parent who has to bury a child than knowing their child loved the Lord and "made the choice" to let Him live in their heart and life. Lee and I have never doubted that Terrence is in more Love than he could have ever known here, had he lived to be 100. But, that never changes the "real" stuff in our daily life that we fight through.

Into our third year of losing Terrence, around my 52nd birthday, I realized a new word in my journey. Separation. It's not a word I am at all fond of, but I know it well, and it suddenly made sense as part of the frayed tapestry of my "life' quilt that was forever changed on December 20, 2008. Oh, I have my quilt, but it has a few more holes than it did when I started the journey. I'm sure before I'm done there will be more holes, tears and tatters.

Terrence was such fun and loved life!

In the nights that sleep didn't come after Terrence died (and, I actually didn't want it to), I knew the truth. As I was feeling so lost without Terrence, it meant that he was at "home." The Lord clearly told me that Terrence's absence from us, here on Earth, couldn't be more real in eternity. He was there, in the

Father's house, feasting at the banqueting table, loved and being loved.

I struggle with the truth that Terrence is more alive than he has ever been. He is living "Forever" and the "Terr hole" in my heart will not be healed until I am in Heaven, too. That is hard, some days unbearable, and others tolerable, but there is always the promise from the Father that I will see Jesus, Terrence, and all my friends and family gone before me one day soon.

I want to be clear that I am so happy for Terrence and the choices he made that led him Home. My human mind, emotions, and broken heart struggle with knowing Terrence is alive. I don't know the form or the "how" of it all, but he is alive. I have asked God so many times (I can't even count how many times), that if Terrence is that alive, could I please see him for just a second? One little second?

God knows me too well, and He knows if I got a peek into Forever, if He parted the clouds and gave me a glimpse, I'd try crawling through the hole in the sky and want to stay. It isn't that I don't embrace my life and all that is here for me to accomplish yet, but there is a broken, sad, and empty place in my life without Terrence that makes me want to see him so desperately.

Terrence was a treasure in a world of so many lost and searching people. He knew his place, his anchor in this life and he knew how to daily be "Jesus this side of Heaven." He made mistakes. He wasn't perfect, but God loved Terrence and knew my son by name.

"SEE I HAVE ENGRAVED YOU ON THE PALMS OF MY HANDS." ISAIAH 49:16 (NIV)

We all need to rest into the truth and promises that are ours to cling to this side of Heaven. Many days these promises are what help one to hang on and get from "moment to moment."

It is a mystery to me how as a mother there is no greater joy or love to be felt than to bear a child. I remember being so excited through my pregnancies with both of the boys. The sheer joy by their mere existence was palpable.

I miss the "smell" of Terrence.

We have personal things that were Terrence's, and I found some in the closet of our upstairs. I could smell Terrence on them. I just fell to the floor sobbing uncontrollably, longing for him. I have been aware of that sweaty, natural, woodsy scent of Terrence several times since he died.

A couple times under our carport, where on his way home to his house, he would turn, look at me, and say, "I love you," and then leave me with one of his sweet smiles.

I long for that smile and a hug like no one else can give me. If you haven't lost a child, parent, or spouse, you probably don't realize the little things that trigger your memory. I can at times remember the "baby" smell of baby wash and lotion as clearly as if I was holding a baby now.

When I feel I am at the "point of no return" in my grief and I cannot go another moment, I am mindful of Mary. I can see her running along the lines of people who watched Jesus carry his cross to Golgotha. She was desperate to catch a glimpse of her baby, watching the cruelty and the injustice that was her son's to bear, with a mother's crushed heart and realizing there was nothing she could do.

I can relate to the gripping fear, panic and need to just see him. I am driven to tears by the love that was hers for those years. Jesus, my salvation, had a mom who cried, mourned, loved, dreamed, hoped and had to watch her child die, a death beyond human comprehension. A Father sat on a throne, knowing the hour was near, the prophecy would be fulfilled, loving deeper than any human emotion or intent.

As scripture documents, this was not an accident or misunderstanding. This was a choice. A choice that was made by a man named Jesus who would carry the world's sin to Calvary. With every nail driven into his body, so were my sins nailed there, too.

Over the years of walking this journey of grief and loss, I have wondered about the choices we have the opportunity to make every day. Choices we make will effect the course of our lives. It is easy to get consumed with the routine, mundane things of this life. Death has a way of rearranging every priority that we thought we had. Life as we saw it becomes cloudy, overwhelming and hard to even think in that sense. All that I had known for so long was changed forever and nothing looked the same.

The simple tasks of a routine for me were unconquerable at best for months.

As I mentioned earlier, Lee and I took only about a week off after Terrence's service. It was difficult at first. I managed to hide my grief, buck up, put on my best "Christian" face and garment for the day.

Act a part.

Get through the play for the day and go behind closed doors and have a piece of me die with the setting sun.

It was this routine for many months and into the second year of our grief. In the weeks and first months after Terrence died, my body physically shut down, too. I have found now, going through the years after Terrence's passing, that this is a pattern, and my body does what it wants, for months. Physically, there was and is a trauma that takes on a life of its own it seems.

Through it all, there is never a moment that we are not loved, cared for, and every provision for our needs being met. God continues to shower us with every good and perfect gift designed just for Lee and me. We have learned to step back, embrace each blessing lavished upon us and not take any of it for granted.

As many family, friends, and acquaintances we know have also lost loved ones. they can and will tell us, "Life is short. Today is your gift, so don't take it for granted."

We have known heartache, grief and joy in ways we would never have thought possible. It is not by anything we do or can orchestrate that brings the best and worst to life. It is by a Heavenly Father who knows the hairs on our head.

There is no greater love than a Father who gives His Son to save a condemned world. How amazing it is to me that there is a love so true, pure, never-ending, constant, unconditional, and free and mine…

"JESUS WAS BORN CRUCIFIED. WHENEVER HE BECAME CONSCIOUS OF WHOM HE WAS HE ALSO BECAME CONSCIOUS OF WHAT HE HAD TO DO. THE CROSS-SHAPED SHADOW COULD ALWAYS BE SEEN. AND THE SCREAMS OF HELL'S IMPRISONED COULD ALWAYS BE HEARD."

THIS EXPLAINS THE GLINT OF DETERMINATION ON HIS FACE AS HE TURNED TO GO TO JERUSALEM FOR THE LAST TIME. HE WAS ON HIS DEATH MARCH." LUKE 9:51

SO CALL IT WHAT YOU WISH; AN ACT OF GRACE. A PLAN OF REDEMPTION. A MARTYR'S SACRIFICE. BUT WHATEVER YOU CALL IT, DON'T CALL IT AN ACCIDENT. IT WAS NOTHING BUT."

Grace for the Moment
by Max Lucado

I am left without words when I can accept and know that it wasn't an angry mob; it wasn't the ropes on his wrists or the soldiers who forced him to Calvary's hill. It was love that hung Jesus on the cross. Had there been no betrayal, a cowardly Pilot or a mob crying, "Crucify him; let Barabbas go free," Jesus would have still freely walked that hill to Calvary. Even if he would have had to nail his own feet and hands, he would have; that was his destiny.

When I ponder the love, purpose and hope that is mine through Jesus, it is more than I can comprehend and allow myself to freely accept. His love and forgiveness are ours free. The only thing He asks is to believe.

"For God so loved the world that He gave His one and only Son, that whosoever believes in Him shall not perish but have eternal life."
John 3:16 (NIV)

Chapter 4
Death is Ugly

"He will wipe every tear from their eyes. There will be no more death or mourning or crying or pain, for the old order of things has passed away." Revelation 21:4 (NIV)

Every one of us, sometime in life, has encountered death of some sort. I remember the first funeral I went to was my cousin's. I was very close to her, and I believe she was about 11 years old. I had never seen anyone in a coffin before, and it was something I will never forget.

Death is a mystery, an ugly process. Whatever words we use, death is ugly. That is, in the physical realm. The body has stopped living. The chest doesn't rise and fall. There's no pulse, no heartbeat. All visible signs of life are gone. Oh, but what life begins with that last earthly breath!

"I TELL YOU THE TRUTH; HE WHO BELIEVES HAS EVERLASTING LIFE." JOHN 6:47 (NIV)

What an amazing promise. All we have to do is believe and we will spend forever in eternity, and we will see our loved ones there.

When we were at the hospital for those few hours, Terrence was fighting the sepsis attacking his body. The battle raging inside his body was so obvious. He had gone into a diabetic coma; he had a fever of 107 degrees; he was breathing so rapidly and fighting against the toxins that were attacking his internal organs.

His internal specialist believes Terrence could have survived the diabetes (which none of us, not even Terrence, were aware he had until he was hospitalized.) The doctor also felt there was an internal injury (probably his appendix) which is where the sepsis gained access, continuing through his blood stream, poisoning his entire body and every vital organ along the way.

"AS LONG AS WE ARE AT HOME IN THE BODY WE ARE AWAY FROM THE LORD." II CORINTHIANS 5:6 (NIV)

I watched my son fighting to live. I watched the doctors and staff doing everything they knew to do to save lives. It is all very clear, this side of it, that Terrence was fighting for his life. I prayed, believing and asking for a miracle. Never once did I let the idea of death come into my mind. My son was 29. He loved life. Life loved him. He had his whole future ahead of him, including all his mom's dreams for him….so much waiting to be fulfilled.

I did not want to leave my baby lying in the hospital alone. Everything maternal within me was kicking into overdrive. I remember trying so hard to get from that waiting area back into Terrence's room upon learning he was gone. I needed to spend some time with him before they transported Terrence's body to the funeral home. I kept fainting. I was quite embarrassed, but eventually I made it to his bedside.

When I got there, I felt peace that rested on me like a blanket. He was so peaceful, so quiet. Colors were changing in his face and hands, but he was so peaceful. He was with Jesus; he was being embraced by the Father and welcomed "Home." I just had to find a way to get through those moments with him that went so very fast. Lee and I were the last ones to leave Terrence and that hospital. My sisters were there walking out with us. That was the longest walk to our vehicle in the parking lot. I kept looking to his window, to the hallway. I just knew Terrence would be there waving at us. To say the least, we were numb, in disbelief, reeling, shocked, and not wanting to accept what had just taken place in less than 24 hours.

As we left the hospital, heading home, without Terrence, I knew it was a pivotal point in my life—changing me forever. It is easy to profess God's faithfulness and love when everything is going right in your life. It is entirely different to have those beliefs remain the same in the darkest hours of life. I have never doubted God's love for me and I strongly clung to what I believed. Never had God's love become as tangible to me as in the hours and weeks that would follow.

I look back, and if I could do it differently, I would have never left his side. I would have prayed unceasingly at his bedside. So many things I know I would have done differently. The truth always is quickened in my spirit, my mind and my heart. God was always in control, never left his throne, and the preparations that were being made for Terrence's "coming home" party never stopped for a second.

I remember running into a good friend Christmas Eve afternoon in a local mall. He and his son were doing last minute Christmas shopping. I was looking for something to wear to Terrence's funeral, and from the mall we were headed to the funeral home for "the viewing."

Those days after Terrence died were such a blur, compelled by obligation and plans that had to be made. I had made up my mind standing in the hall of the hospital, knowing I had to leave Terrence there, that I didn't want anyone to doubt God's plan for Terrence and for us as a family.

I wanted nothing more than Terrence's death to be a testimony of love, healing, restoration, his love of Jesus and of hope.

The morning before we went to the viewing, I remember meeting at our home with our pastor who was doing Terrence's service. Lyndsay, her sister-in-law, Lee and I were gathered with Pastor Rick. I can still see Lyndsay, preoccupied, and I was unsure what she was thinking. Then some time into the "planning process" I figured it out. That dear girl wanted to see her husband, the first time since leaving him in that hospital room four days earlier. She wanted to be there with him, to spend any time that she could before having to let him go forever, until Heaven. As a mom, there is no greater joy than knowing that your child had love in his life and was happy. Thank you, Jesus, and thank you, Lyndsay.

It is beyond anything you can ever think possible, to stand at the side of a coffin and see your child so lifeless, cold, not smiling, talking, or laughing. But as I stood there I had such a peace wash over me in that little viewing room, just as I had in the hospital room. There was a tangible presence that rested wherever Terrence was—the peace of Jesus, the hope of Heaven and forever in eternity with our Heavenly Father. And, Terrence was there.

"PEACE I LEAVE WITH YOU; MY PEACE I GIVE YOU. I DO NOT GIVE TO YOU AS THE WORLD GIVES. DO NOT LET YOUR HEARTS BE TROUBLED AND DO NOT BE AFRAID." JOHN 14:27 (NIV)

I don't remember feeling fear and haven't since, but there was the unfathomable reality of living for years without Terrence. It was and is still hard to look forward and not have pain in my heart. As time propels me on, I realize that there will always be pain, some days easier to bear than others; but God still has me tucked under His wings of healing.

I go to the cemetery often and there is no other place that I find the peace that rests with me when I am there. A well-known author once said, "If you have any major decisions that need made, go to a cemetery to make them."

I am a true believer of that, as much confusion and heaviness is lifted when I spend time at Terrence's grave. Oh, I know as a Christian, he's not there, so to speak, but I also know that as his mom, he has never been more there!

I can remember when we sat graveside, preparing to commit Terrence's body. All I could think was how could I get under the casket and go with Terrence. Until you have been in that place of grief, loss and brokenness, there is no way to make it look or sound pretty. Death is ugly.

But I have also walked into my eighth year of losing my son, knowing that death is just the beginning for the one who has died and those of us left behind.

The process of death, in any form, is nothing more than life being robbed from a loved one. It is also the sovereign plan of God that the life of our son stopped on that December morning in 2008.

We had no way of knowing the hours we were in

the middle of, were the last hours we would have with Terrence. But that is how it is supposed to be, according to Kingdom dynamics. His word speaks of the things that we won't understand and mysteries that aren't ours to know. I can tell you what a day it is going to be when I stand before my God. What a glorious day that will be.

It is natural and expected to a degree, to be consumed with grief and to feel detached from all that was so important before losing your loved one. The consuming thoughts of life without those we love so dearly and the plans that were dashed and buried with their body. I know for me there was so much yet to be done with Terrence's life and so many people who would get to know him, that it was and is at times, still difficult to let those "things" of this life go.

Lee and I both struggle when out shopping or dining, and we see parents treating their children badly. There was an incident not long after Terrence died where Lee and I were eating out and someone who appeared to be the dad came in with three sweet looking boys.

The adult man was never soft or kind during ordering their food or waiting. He was hard and quick to snap at the boys. I couldn't help but notice that one of the older boys, maybe seven years old walked behind coming into the restaurant and did the same when leaving. It was all I could do to stay seated and not address the man with those children.

When you lose a child, you can get caught in the trap of feeling, "I've been robbed," and getting angry with those who have children that you think they don't deserve. There was and still are at times, a repenting that has to be done on my part. I pray for the children I see who I believe to be victims of their circumstances, deserving Godly parents. I am reminded that I am to be Jesus here and now, not to judge.

And he said,

"I TELL YOU THE TRUTH, UNLESS YOU CHANGE AND BECOME LIKE LITTLE CHILDREN, YOU WILL NEVER ENTER THE KINGDOM OF HEAVEN. THEREFORE, WHOEVER HUMBLES HIMSELF LIKE THIS CHILD IS THE GREATEST IN THE KINGDOM OF HEAVEN. AND WHOEVER WELCOMES A LITTLE CHILD LIKE THIS IN MY NAME WELCOMES ME." MATTHEW 18:3-5 (NIV)

How interesting it is then, that those children that we spend years teaching, training, and grooming into societal individuals, at their core are young, innocent, trustworthy, loving and trusting. They are what we are to become like to enter the Kingdom.

God is such a wise God. I have always been intrigued by children, their purity and innocence, their absolute sheer delight with the simplest of things of life and their unconditional love. I remember hearing or reading somewhere that the purest thing that we can ever experience is to hold a newborn and breathe in that sweetness of their first breaths.

We were blessed on March 2, 2016 to have our first grandchild, a precious little girl. Her name is Raegan Marie Skinner, and she is a calm, peaceful baby that has her parents and grandparents seeing the world in a whole different light. She is the most perfect, innocent blessing who we have had the privilege of loving so completely and deeply in some time. We love see the redeeming power of God in Raegan, bathed in such indescribable joy and love. She is a perfect and precious gift from God, entrusted to Chase and Stephanie to love, protect and enjoy every day.

I am looking so forward to Heaven, seeing so many loved ones, young and old in their perfected bodies as they were created to be even before their birth.

It is so easy to get your vision and hopes ripped from your life when death comes. There is an end to all that was so alive and so loved in this life. Choosing to profess and know in your knower that our loved ones live in ways that we have to just wait to see, as well as experience for ourselves.

One of the nights that I couldn't sleep, roaming the house I ended up in the kitchen standing in front of the refrigerator looking at the pictures of Terrence

I have placed there. It was raining and windy outside; I could hear the rain on the covered decks and the chimes off the kitchen deck.

I was snapped out of my thoughts, and I panicked thinking Terrence was alone, cold and out in the rain and wind. I had to be with him! Then I realized it was the middle of the morning and only I would be comforted to be near him. It was so real and so urgent that I go be with Terrence, the tears rolled down my cheeks, soaking my robe. I was comforted with the knowledge that Terrence was safe, loved, warm, and in light I couldn't even begin to imagine.

Those first trips to the cemetery found me sobbing, mourning, beyond any other human emotion I have ever experienced.

Mourning is a "process" that I will never be 'through' or 'over', but it has eased some.

The first weeks, I put on my mom hat, pruning back dead flowers in the arrangements, picking up debris, keeping all neat and in order on the grave. Numb, broken, lost and yet doing what needed to be done to ease the pain for Lyndsay, Lee, Chase, anyone who would visit Terrence's grave in those early days.

Those first visits, I just knew Terrence was going to be a modern day miracle and come back to life. As time has progressed, I know my grief was so unbearable, unthinkable, it was my way of "coping" with the knowledge my son laid in that fresh dirt. The downside of that hoping, in the flesh, was the bottomless lows I would hit.

As I am writing, I will tell you that driving away from the cemetery is still difficult and the tears flow…there are days, time frames, that I can't account for; weeks turning into months while I screamed for it all to stop and if only just for a minute, for me to have Terrence. I needed to hug him, smell him, touch him, and to tell him I loved him and that he was an amazing son and man of God.

I needed to say how proud I was of him, how much he had shown me Jesus in his life, how he had challenged me to be a better person and to see the good in people.

I miss his infectious laughter, his amazing ability to turn an everyday event into a story. I wanted to thank him for loving me unconditionally, for being a great friend and son to his dad, an amazing brother to Chase, a good husband to Lyndsay, a thoughtful co-worker and staff member in a job where he shined.

There was so much I wanted to tell him and God constantly reminds me that Terrence knows all of it, and so much more. Most of what I have mentioned, I did get to say so many times to Terrence when he was alive. He knew he was loved; I told him daily when I would talk to him and any time I would see him. He was good at giving a big hug when he would leave our house, or wherever we were, and he'd say, "I love you, Moms." We were so blessed in this life, and he knew he was loved. We told him.

Many times at his grave, I tell my sweet boy who sleeps there, how much I miss him and forever will love him. How much everyone who knew him misses him. A great friend of Terrence's shared with me how during their Christmas his dad had just stopped in the middle of all that was going on and said, "You know, I sure miss Terrence."

I catch myself even now thinking, "This is a terrible dream. This cannot be my life, to continue without Terrence."

I can go through the house for days, and then one day I stop and look at one of the pictures I have on the walls, and I cry uncontrollably. What may be fine to see or think about one day may be what sends me into the tears that I think will never stop the next.

The Comforter continues to hold me tightly until it passes, and we move forward—from glory to glory is my desire.

As I mentioned earlier, a good friend of mine, Jean, passed away the July before Terrence. I remember her saying she was frightened of dying. She knew the Lord, loved Jesus, and was one of the most influential people who encouraged me and loved me into the Kingdom.

I miss her so much, but I know that Terrence and she are happier and healthier than they ever could have been on earth. Many times I have said, "Death is a journey we all are going to take. Now the means and the suffering is going to be different for each of us." We cannot see Jesus and spend forever with God if we don't die. It's that simple.

I've seen that death is no respecter of person; it calls on whoever it wishes. However, I do know an absolute truth—God has prepared a place for those who love and serve Him. We humans forget that we were not created to last forever. Plastic surgeons, drugs and beauty products are only a temporary fix to our "terminal" diagnosis. Oh, certainly we look better, years younger, have hair again, and probably feel better, but the end result is inevitable. We all die.

I remember those days, weeks, months that have turned into years, as I walk out my "season of mourning," how I feel panic with my loved ones.

When Chase traveled very far, I became anxious at where he was going, when he would be home, how long he was going to be away. If someone felt ill, that gripping fear of "not knowing" rips at my very heart—rushing back with all of the shock and unbelief of a disease undiagnosed or not treated "soon enough."

There was guilt in those early hours and days after Terrence died. Lee and I really struggled with and we still do, not reading the signs that Terrence was diabetic. We didn't know. I lived with a diabetic, how could I have not seen signs?

There was a terrible storm with snow here in Oregon the days before Terrence died. He and Lyndsay commuted together to another city to work. There was no school where Terrence was a teacher's assistant, and Lyndsay didn't have to go to work either for the Monday and Tuesday before Terrence went into the hospital.

That Monday I had all of my kids here at home with Lee and me. We made applesauce. A dear sweet friend had given us apples, and I had been procrastinating with the last box or so.

Terrence said, "Mom, we're going to get those apples done."

So, we all worked in the kitchen making applesauce. It was the best memory for me, and the last picture of Terrence I have, earth side. That was Terrence, motivate and encourage me into "getting it done." We had so much fun together. How I miss all of those times together.

We were and still are a very close family. Even death couldn't tear us apart, in our hearts any way. Lyndsay moved a month after Terrence's funeral. Chase and Stephanie moved eight miles further away from us, and I was feeling death all over again. Both of the boys and their spouses lived here in Halsey, Oregon, just blocks from Lee and me. I was the happiest mama chick ever. I had the chicks close to the coop.

When Lyndsay moved away, and Chase and Stephanie moved to a new home, I was feeling death and separation all over. It is hard to explain in words, but I remember that lost, silent, lonely feeling so clearly. Death takes on many forms.

I not only experienced physical death, but I also saw futures, hopes, Terrence and Lyndsay's future, grandchildren, all not to be. I always have had this dream of being Grandma just down the street and the grandkids all ride their bikes to Grandma's house. That dream was crushed.

Now, I am eternally grateful for Chase and Stephanie. I have so many hopes, dreams and plans with them. I could not be where I am today if not for my kids, Lee, family, friends, and for so many just knowing us and who loved Terrence. I know my life is such a gift. I have so much for which to be thankful.

God continues to bless and minister His goodness to us. I write of the "plans and dreams" as a family unit that were crushed for me.

Life goes on, all around us, and it is difficult to be a part of it when all you want to do is to die yourself. I just want the pain to stop, my mind to stop replaying everything that I think I could have done differently.

Silence comes at the most awkward times.

People don't know what to say to you. The medical forms ask how many live births. The list goes on and on. There is a part of life that continues relentlessly and seems very cruel. When we went out after Terrence died (in the planning stages before his service), I remember thinking, "Why is everyone so normal. Don't they know?" Of course, they didn't know and that is how death is.

Everyone doesn't know and life goes on, as awful as it is for those who grieve. The world continues turning. Terrence dying just before Christmas was excruciating. I had most of his gifts and just needed a few more things. I knew he was going to love his Oregon Ducks slippers—he was a Duck fan to the bone. I had taken time off after Christmas to be with him, and he was excited for that.

There were a couple bills I had to pay the Monday after Terrence went to Jesus, and I later heard one of the places couldn't believe I was out paying bills. I wasn't sure who they wanted to pay them for me? Going into stores to finish Christmas shopping was awful. Everyone was so happy and excited for the holidays. Not me. I had to just stop shopping and leave the stores. It was more than I could handle.

Although I was so sad, couldn't breathe or stop crying at times, I was comforted with the knowledge that Terrence was spending Christmas with the Christmas. He was having endless love and joy lavished on him, and we were just going through the motions, to make decisions, and glorify God while giving honor to Terrence.

The only concern I had regarding Terrence's funeral was honoring God number one, and giving Terrence the honor he deserved. He was a godly man; he loved his wife, his family and friends, his co-workers and students, and just life in general.

He didn't have a problem being "Jesus" in a lost world. He knew how to be accepting, understanding, compassionate, and an incredibly gifted listener. He had an amazing sense of humor. He brought such joy to me that there are days I don't know if I can do this journey, long-term, without him. But I do, and I am.

When you are blessed with children who are good people, contributors to society, and most importantly who love the Lord, there is no greater joy for you as a parent.

A family friend shared with me, "There is just nothing like the relationship of a mother and her son." I am blessed beyond measure with the children who God loaned to me. I know they are the Father's gifts to me. When I am given a priceless gift, I love to just look at it. That is how I was and still am with my kids, Chase and his wife, Stephanie.

They are amazing people who make this world a better place. As clearly as I know we all will die, I know we will pass from death to life as we have never experienced it before—the wholeness that will be ours and the loved ones who we will see again! There are days I just want to go now. Yet, I know God has all of my days well in his hands.

I awake with praise for the new day. (Well, most of the time.) And, I go to bed with thanksgiving for all God has trusted me to accomplish that day.

That first summer we were struggling with spring coming and knowing summer would find us grasping at an empty chair on the patio. We spent hours on those decks just talking and solving a lot of life "stuff" as a family. One June day, I decided to go outside and try to just spend some time out there. I was sitting on the deck crying at the empty chair across from me, when a hummingbird came through the adjoining deck, and stopped in mid-air straight across from me above "Terrence's chair" and just hovered.

It was probably only seconds that it hovered there, but in those seconds I was given a "sign" that all of us were going to be just fine, and that Terrence couldn't be more alive than he was at that moment. I felt the same overwhelming peace that afternoon on the deck as I had in Terrence's hospital room when he had gone to Heaven. Since that hummingbird encounter, numerous others have followed, usually in the late spring and across those same desks, crossing Terrence's chair.

"THOSE WHO WALK UPRIGHTLY ENTER INTO PEACE; THEY FIND REST AS THEY LIE IN DEATH." ISAIAH 57:2 (NIV)

I believe Terrence was an example of the above mentioned scripture. He did his best to walk uprightly and there was a peace he had, as well as peace that rested on him in death.

"LIFE ONLY DEMANDS FROM YOU THE STRENGTH YOU POSSESS. ONLY ONE FEAT IS POSSIBLE—NOT TO HAVE RUN AWAY."

Dag Hammarskjold

Many who saw and have seen Lee and me walk out our grief daily, have said, "There is such a peace and calm you have. How do you do it?"

Even at Terrence's funeral, those who were gathered at the home going service, friends, family, and those who loved Terrence, were amazed that we could stand behind our son's casket and share with such vulnerability and honesty.

We have only God to thank for a peace that passes all understanding, as well as, grace, hope and comfort that only comes from God. If people sense you are being honest and "keeping it real" as Terrence was fond of saying, they are at peace and encouraged. We desire to show the tremendous hope and blessings that we have been given and shown since Terrence's death. Many times it is as simple as Hammarskjold says, "Let the grief flow and display the utmost courage that you possess at the time."

"Peace I leave with you; my peace I give you. I don't give to you as the world gives." John 14:27

There is a peace that comes from the Father's heart that is like no one has ever experienced. I can testify to this first hand. There are so many days that I didn't think I could step another step, nor did I have the desire to do so. But, as a Father tends to his children, providing for them and assuring that all of their needs are met, the Heavenly Father comes with such gentleness, kindness, love and hope to my rescue.

I have always been intrigued and overwhelmed at how the Father stands, ready, always, waiting, for us to call out to him and I am sure it is all he can do not to rush to our aid without being asked!

Chapter 5
Eternity Is Real

"FOR GOD SO LOVED THE WORLD THAT HE GAVE HIS ONE AND ONLY SON, THAT WHOEVER BELIEVES IN HIM SHALL NOT PERISH BUT HAVE ETERNAL LIFE." JOHN 3:16 (NIV)

There has never been a time that I have been more aware of Heaven and eternity than when I lost Terrence. I saw Heaven opened before my eyes, many times, heard clearly from the Father his promises and plans for me. Never once did I, or have I since, doubted that Terrence is safely Home in the arms of love, forever.

We were in the Critical Care area waiting when the nurse came to the cafeteria and told us they were doing CPR on Terrence—his heart had stopped. We all hurried back upstairs and were waiting there. Lyndsay went to be with Terrence immediately, I waited! I remember as I waited, praying for a miracle, and hearing the Father say, "He's coming home to be with me, I want you to know that."

When the nurse returned, with urgency in her actions she wanted someone "strong" to go back and be with Lyndsay. I knew straight from the throne of God that Terrence was dying. I had the split second decision to make and decide if I wanted to go and be with him as he died. I couldn't do it. I couldn't move. Everything went black; it made no sense, yet made complete sense.

My sweet boy was going to be with Jesus. My sister stood in for me, holding Terrence's wife.

There is nothing in our humanness that can prepare us for the death of someone we love. As a Christian, I know Heaven is real. I believe in life after death. I know we stand before the throne of God and are welcomed home. We will see all of our loved ones who loved the Lord and are there already.

I am keenly aware of the reality of life after death—eternity. There is not one thing in "this life" that has made that so real to me as knowing Terrence was gone. Then my real faith test came. Truly believing what I had heard, read, been taught and believed for myself about life after death and Heaven.

As a little girl, I knew there was a Heaven; it was above the clouds. I went to Vacation Bible School and had an older generation family that loved the Lord. Somewhere along the line I had heard or been told about Heaven. I just knew it was real. I went to church when I was in Junior High and somewhere in that period of my life, there was a revelation of my need for Him in my life.

I attended a Nazarene Church in our hometown for some years and during my sophomore or junior year in high school I made a choice to surrender my life to the Lord. Now at that age there is so much pressure, and for me personally, there was the fear of having to "change" my life. It wasn't as difficult as I made it out to be, but there were challenges, nonetheless.

I met my husband the next year after I graduated. We dated for about four months, got engaged, and were married eight months after our first date. It did seem fast for some people, but I loved him (What I knew about love then!) I remember my father-in-law asking me after we showed him my engagement ring, "Are you sure you know what you're doing?" How funny now 33 years of marriage later; I do chuckle at times.

That was his same question when roughly seven weeks after I said, "I do," I was pregnant. I wanted Terrence desperately. It was only natural to start our "perfect little family." Never once thinking of how long I would get to keep that perfect little gift in my life—it was a given. We'd see him grow, marry, have his own kids, and we would get to grow old with him and his kids.

Funny, the things you see as important in those early years of marriage, how they influence your

Chase and Terrence on a fishing boat off the Oregon coast.

decisions. Now keep in mind there is not one time, ever, that I didn't want either of my boys. They are two of my most accomplished works in this life and I love them eternally.

I never once thought about not having my boys with me through my life, and they would always have their mom around to help guide them in their lives. Everything is so new and exciting in those early years. I wasn't thinking on "eternal" terms in any form.

Early on in Lee's and my marriage, we began to lose those whom we loved so dearly. It is absolutely unbelievable when I count the saints who are with Terrence now and who were there long before him. The many we had to walk away from at the cemetery.

The spring before Terrence died, we lost a great, dear neighbor that I had grown to love dearly. Three months after our sweet neighbor's passing, my best friend went home to Jesus. Three months after my friend, a family friend and brother to Lee went to Jesus. Terrence went to Jesus less than three months after our family friend. We were pretty "gutted" by the end of 2008. Within eight months' time frame we lost four of the dearest people our family had known and loved as equally as I had.

In all four of those precious lives that ended in 2008, there is not one second that I questioned where they were. Obviously all of them had a physical resting place, but they were "home." They are in eternal health, wholeness, happiness, and love, waiting for us to be with them.

All of us are an amazing gift from the ultimate Creator but we also are created how he "wired" us. I am regularly reminded of the master plan there is for all of us, long before there was "us."

"BEFORE I FORMED YOU IN THE WOMB I KNEW YOU; BEFORE YOU WERE BORN I SET YOU APART." JEREMIAH 1:4 (NIV)

Not long ago I read a book which I cannot remember the title but the author was writing of the spirit that was created for each of us before our birth. Now, that is a Creator who knows what he is doing!

"I WRITE THESE THINGS TO YOU WHO BELIEVE IN THE NAME OF THE SON OF GOD SO THAT YOU MAY KNOW THAT YOU HAVE ETERNAL LIFE." I JOHN 5:13 (NIV)

As I get older and have various encounters in my life that challenge my faith, I am continually being shown my "spirit man," well, spirit woman. There is a very real part of me that will live on forever, in the eternal plans of God and with God.

We have all read or seen the documentary on "after life experiences" and watched intently on every account or retelling. I personally have had the privilege of seeing that Heaven is real.

It was in 2002 I believe (I cannot find the journal that I wrote it into to validate the year) when the "exchange" did happen. I was at my workplace, didn't feel good, and experienced pain in my left arm and up my neck. I called the doctor office that I went to and the receptionist told me to come right in. Lee also worked in the same building, so I found him and he drove me.

We had about a 12-mile drive to the clinic. In those miles I remember a feeling of absence. When we reached the first town, Harrisburg, and we were approaching the traffic signal, I clearly remember feeling "outside" of me and having a second person view of what was going on. It was only for seconds but it seemed so much longer.

I told Lee, "Tell the boys I love them, and I love you, too." He was frantic, and told me I was not going anywhere. I could see us crossing the railroad tracks, driving west toward the traffic lights, but I could also see completely clear skies on the western horizon. I saw huge, golden gates and just inside was a dear friend who passed away of cancer, standing there smiling with her long black curly hair. She was waiting for me.

I remember the exchanges with the Father and asking Him, "What would Lee do and what about the boys?"

I heard, "Taken care of."

I heard me asking, "What would I wear?" (Yeah, only me!)

I heard, "Taken care of."

I asked "Why now? And what would everyone else who knew me do without me?"

"Taken care of."

I remember asking, "What about grandkids? They'll need me."

"Taken care of."

I asked, "What about the clinic, they're not prepared for anything major with the heart."

"Taken care of."

Keep in mind this seemed likes hours to me, but in reality was probably a very brief few minutes. I remember as I felt me "watching" this unfold, there was warmth that I cannot put into words. It was not like a blanket, a warm bath or a great hug from someone. It was beyond anything I have ever felt. The "atmosphere" I was a part of was peaceful and I could feel myself being wrapped in a love that I had never known in this life or have ever felt since.

While these exchanges were happening, I heard, clearly, audibly, "They need you."

We were by now through the first town and headed toward the clinic. I felt a "sliding" back into my seat and a conscious presence of Lee driving and still being en route to the clinic. I knew I was going to be OK, and there was no need to rush or hurry. I had just been told, "They need you." It was not Lee talking to me. I was OK.

I know that I was given that experience to let me know there was nothing to fear; to feel something literally "out of this world," to know beyond a doubt that I have nothing to fear. It also has given me comfort over the years of losing loved ones to know the place and atmosphere they are a part of; I felt it firsthand. I just never knew that it was going to be an encounter that I would draw on, desperately, in the days and sleepless nights that would come.

I have shared with very few people my "dying" experience, but it seems appropriate to do so at this time. I am telling it as what I know from my glimpse of eternity.

I have mentioned in an early chapter that Heaven became real on levels beyond my human comprehension in the last few years, but I also know it is God's mercy and grace he showered me with daily.

I remember hearing on *Focus on the Family* when Dr. Dobson was still hosting, a guest on the show who had lost his wife and children. I believe it was a car accident and the father was the only survivor. Dr. Dobson asked, "How do you make it through each day? How do you keep on living?" The gentlemen said, "James, there is a day coming, I will stand before the throne of God and all of this questioning, heartache and loss will become clear. I will say, 'Oh that is why.'"

I have thought of that radio broadcast so many times over the years since hearing it. How quickly all of our "whys" will be answered, our tears won't matter, we won't feel any more pain or separation by death. In the twinkling of an eye, it will all make sense.

The following is also evidence to me of Heaven and where Terrence is. It was given to Lee and me by a dear family friend, and a friend who stuck closer than a brother to Terrence. Some of the wording has changed from the original hand-written recollection for the purpose of clarifying or making it easier to read. The dialogue as I remember it and the details described are just as I was able to recount it the next day.

December 4, 2010

I decided to write, because I had a dream last night. I wanted to record it, lest I forget it.

I fell asleep and was suddenly standing in a great cathedral. I thought I was in Saint Peter's in Rome, until I realized that Saint Peter's or any other structure built by human hands could not and never could be as vast, expansive and gloriously adorned with simply complex features and light as this place where I found myself.

All around me people were walking in pairs. Old walked and happily talked with old; young with young; old with young; men with men; women with women; and women with men. There was but a simple similarity with every twosome. One individual wore everyday clothing, while the other wore a red (blood red) jacket or robe. All looked well, healthy, strong and happy.

I noticed a great wide staircase so grand and tall that even though it was gently sloping, I could not see where it ended. Pairs were ascending and talking as they rose higher and higher with each step. I felt drawn to join the club, though I had no partner. As I took my first step, I realized that I was wearing a red robe and instantly there beside me was my dearest friend, Terrence. He looked strong, healthy and more filled with life than I had ever seen. We fell into lock-step together without so much as a stutter and began to climb. All others around us were no longer there. They had become invisible to our eyes as we climbed faster than I would ever imagine possible.

"Pope! You came to walk with me the rest of the way."

"Yeah, I did Terrence." The "rest of the way" to where and what I didn't know. I was somewhat confused, but our conversation was casual, as if we had just seen each other yesterday.

Finally, we reached the top of the staircase and entered into a massive and seemingly empty balcony, where we sat beside each other and talked.

"Where we do we go from here, Terrence?"

"Home."

"You know, bud, a lot of people are going to be very upset with you. You've been gone so long, without so

much as a word. We had a funeral and everything."

"That's okay, dude. I can handle it. But yeah, I've been gone awhile."

"So, when are we going home?"

"Soon. It's actually about time to go now." With that, he stood up, and I followed.

When we were both standing I said, "Well, let's get going then," glancing toward the staircase. When I looked back Terrence was standing there smiling. I couldn't understand why he would keep everyone at home waiting any longer. No one had seen him in almost two years and no one had ever seen him so happy, so healthy, as he looked now.

With a peaceful and loving expression that I knew held sadness only for me (and only for a moment) in my misunderstanding, Terrence spoke.

"Home for me is different than it is for you right now. You can't come to my home yet. It will be a little while before we see each other again."

Instant knowledge of that which he was speaking of hit me and gave me both a sense of wondrous awe and a deep heavy sadness. Terrence, standing here before me in his street clothes as he would have been dressed any other day, reached out and drew me into a warm and loving embrace. It was one I had remembered fondly and most clearly.

He said, "It's time to go. I love you brother."

"I love you too, brother."

"See you later, Bud. Take it easy." He said as he stepped away still facing me. He glowed in a way that

increased until a brilliant flash ignited and then went silently out. He was gone.

I turned to walk back down the massive and still ever-glorious staircase. As I stepped on the first stair and started back down to where Terrence and I had come from, I realize that I was not alone. All of the people that I had seen prior to my ascent and pairing were walking down with me, minus their plain-clothed companions. While we had all walked up in pairs, unable to see or hear each other, we who were walking down alone could all see each other again. Though we could see each other, we were all inclined to descend silently, reflectively and with what seemed like a little sadness. We were all visible to each other and we were all wearing the red robes.

As I neared the bottom, a scene similar to what I saw in the very beginning became visible again and as I stepped from the final step downward, I awoke in my bed, both grieving and in awe of what I had witnessed.

What was it that I had witnessed? I do not know. Was I merely dreaming? Perhaps, but I don't think so. It felt so real and so solid. Did I get a glimpse of eternity? Perhaps, but I cannot say for sure. What I do know is that I can still see that place which I cannot in detail describe. Nor would I try to describe it in detail, knowing that my description would fall so incredibly short of the pure glory and power that was in that place, the peace and love that radiate not from that place, but through it, within it and around it. What I do know is that nearly two years later I finally said goodbye and have been able to admit wholeheartedly that I truly, deeply and painfully miss my friend.

Give glory to God in the highest and peace to his people on earth."

Thank you, Brandon, for sharing this with Lee and me. I weep every time I read it, but with a heart that bears witness to everything you experienced. What a gift you were given; I am jealous, wishing it was me, but I am so glad you got to spend some time with Terrence.

He loved you like a brother, and he knew you loved him. What a blessing to walk this side of Heaven in bonds that are only from God.

"BE DEVOTED TO ONE ANOTHER IN BROTHERLY LOVE."
ROMANS 12:10

My boys and me.

Chapter 6
Crazy Things People Say

"A WORD APTLY SPOKEN IS LIKE APPLES OF GOLD IN SETTINGS OF SILVER." PROVERBS 25:11 (NIV)

If only words that were spoken or the words that we speak could be so aptly spoken that they were as apples of gold in silver settings. Unfortunately, we are all human and sometimes our words become inaptly spoken and are like peroxide on an open wound.

Many of the things that were shared with us over the years have been words that were and are seasoned with love. You know what I am going to say next, there were those that are seasoned with Tabasco, they burn and hurt. I don't believe it is on purpose by any means, but I have a whole new perspective on what I say and how I say it, both in grieving and in joy.

One of my all time favorites has to be, "He's in a better place."

I do believe that, I know it is the truth but there

are the days that this does not ease my mother's broken heart. There is no better place that Terrence should be than around the dining room table with us, on the deck in "his" chair, in the living room watching sports with his dad, with his brother and his sister-in-law, with his wife, but those places and things are not to be. The truth of who God is, who we are going to be in Heaven, and what happens to us after we die, is what helps me continue when the clouds roll in and the darkest day falls.

"He's not suffering anymore."

I know that is also true, but I also know that God does miracles, healing like no one can believe or eyes can see. There isn't a single reason that I can think of as to why Terrence shouldn't have been healed, in my way of thinking. The key for me to remember is, it is not up to me to decide who is healed and who is not. It is my choice to believe God to be just, fair and true to everything he has ever shown me or promise he makes in the Bible.

"MANY SEEK AN AUDIENCE WITH A RULER, BUT IT IS FROM THE LORD THAT MAN GETS JUSTICE." PROVERBS 29:26 (NIV)

"He's with his loved ones."

Well, yes, that's also true, but there are a lot of people left behind who loved him more than they ever realized until he was gone! There is such a weight to every "I Love You" we got here, to every "It's all good, Moms." Terrence knew how to love, and he was even better at showing it, and greater yet, saying it. We know how much Terrence loved us and he knew how much we loved him because we said it; we didn't assume it so, we made it so.

There is so much speculation and assumption that happens in times of unexpected death. I remember that word of Terrence's death reached our little hometown before we even got home from the hospital, which was a three- to four-hour time frame from death to our walking into our house.

People mean well; they just don't always know how to verbalize those well-meant intentions. I wasn't ever angry with all of the "talking" that was going on with Terrence's death. It just struck me so odd, that in a world of such turmoil and national catastrophe, that it was an issue of importance to so many. I also know that there were so many people, family, friends and mere acquaintances that Terrence made in the 29 years of his life, that they were as sad and shocked as we were with the news of his death. There is a natural curiosity when death occurs.

As the years have passed there have been so many opportunities to minister the hope of Jesus because of Terrence. God has opened doors, and we have met people in random places and had the privilege of sharing our journey, the hope and love we have.

Our heart is for parents who have lost their child or children. We see that God is using every piece and every part of the death we experienced so deeply and unfathomably as a means to show Jesus. The blessing we have in knowing Terrence loved the Lord, no questioning or wondering. He loved Jesus. What a peace we have in that knowledge and hope that comes with such comfort and peace in your soul which ministers to your mind.

We have a renowned awareness of what we speak out of our mouths being either a blessing or a curse. We have desired and tried desperately to make it blessing.

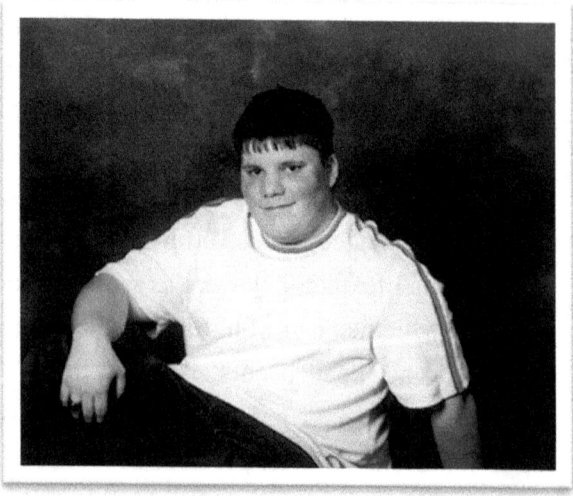

Terrence's senior picture

"PLEASANT WORDS ARE A HONEYCOMB, SWEET TO THE SOUL AND HEALING TO THE BONES." PROVERBS 16:34 (NIV)

Each of us, as the body of Christ, are called to be ambassadors of the Good News, of the hope in Jesus and the truth of his Word. I lived and am living days that are hard to just get out of bed, embrace the day, and move forward, when all I want to do is go backwards in time.

A friend asked me, "What would Terrence want you to do?"

That was an easy answer, but far harder to walk out in every day actions and deeds when your heart is so broken and tender. So many times, more than I can tell, I have heard Terrence say, "It's going to be okay, Moms." I am okay, and I know there are levels of suffering I am protected from that many people are experiencing every day. It doesn't change the situation or circumstances of my suffering. But it makes me appreciative of where I am, and where I am not!

As a parent, there is guilt that accompanies the death of your child. Whether spoken aloud or not, it is still there. They are our child, to love, to raise, to protect no matter how old, married or not. There is such natural remorse, questioning and guilt that we put on ourselves, but it is nothing to the devastation the enemy wants to inflict.

All that God wants and means for good, the enemy and legions of hell work overtime to destroy, to rob and kill. Now my comfort as a Christian is in knowing that my score has been settled and my salvation is solidified with Jesus' death. The enemy could care less what I am thinking or wanting: his goal is for me to end up in hell, no matter what he has to do, and he tries. Greater truth yet is, I am the Lord's. His fingerprints are all over me, and my heart is His forever.

Those who really knew Terrence knew he loved the Lord, and those who knew very little about the faith he had, knew him simply by the life he lead and choices he made. He didn't have to walk and talk his belief; he lived it on a day to day basis, the best he knew how.

Countless conversations have been shared with us in regards to Terrence. Many about his sense of humor, his love for his family, his faith, his love for his wife, his job, coworkers, and so many other details of his life. I think one of the greatest compliments Lee and I have received numerous times, has been, "Terrence didn't just happen to be a great young man who loved the Lord. He had parents who taught him those things." That is one of the most humbling compliments we have heard. To know we did our job as parents in teaching and loving Terrence with the unconditional love we have received is priceless.

Many times we have heard, "You guys were so happy and such a great family." There was guilt and questioning that I had after Terrence died. I wondered and asked if I was too selfish in my "own" sheer joy and comfort of my family, their spouses and all of my own immediate family? It was very difficult those first weeks and months making sense of all the pain I felt and trying to find the "why" in any of it.

Someone once told me that it's OK to ask, "Why?" but be prepared for a lot of the time to have no answer. I have come to understand that in ways I never thought I would or ever wanted to. We are in a world of advance and technology beyond what was ever thought possible, so it doesn't seem that complex to me.

GOD'S WORD ASSURES ME THAT, "AND WE KNOW THAT IN ALL THINGS GOD WORKS FOR THE GOOD OF THOSE WHO LOVE HIM." ROMANS 8:28

I know that our journey is one of those "all things." Mother Teresa has a quote which says, "I know God won't give me more than I can handle, but why does he trust me so much." When I think of this quote I am excited for Heaven, to meet God, and to see what He sees in me, because I don't feel that strong.

Terrence was best man at Chase's wedding. Here he is making a toast and speech.

Chapter 7
We Get to Go

"IN MY FATHER'S HOUSE ARE MANY ROOMS; IF IT WERE NOT SO, I WOULD HAVE TOLD YOU. I AM GOING THERE TO PREPARE A PLACE FOR YOU. AND IF I GO AND PREPARE A PLACE FOR YOU I WILL COME BACK AND TAKE YOU TO BE WITH ME THAT YOU ALSO MAY BE WHERE I AM." JOHN 14:2-3 (NIV)

As small children, most of us are taught that Jesus loves us, and we're going to go to Heaven some day. It is a far cry from what I learned as a child to the reality of burying your son, walking away from a grave with complete confidence knowing he is "in" Heaven. I'm not saying I didn't believe that, I am saying walking out what you believe is different than knowing what you believe. I can tell you what I believe is far less painful than walking it out! I can also say that I would not be the woman of God I am today if it was not for everything God has allowed into my life because he loves me that much.

My husband and I were crying and sharing our tremendous sadness with each other one day, and I said how amazing it is that of all the people God could have chosen for "this" journey, he chose us. All of us have "God unique" journeys we are on, and every one of us is "you-nique." We were formed and fashioned by the Master's handiwork, created in his image, for his glory. There is not another "me" anywhere in the world with the call and destiny that I have.

I had the chance to talk to Terrence on numerous occasions about Heaven. He had a very good friend, Travis, killed in Iraq, which was very hard on Terrence. He loved Travis like a brother, and I know Travis loved Terrence, too. A week or so before Travis' death, Terrence had received a letter from him, as well as others while he was serving in the Army. Terrence held them very dear and precious.

When Terrence started grade school here and the teacher asked, "Who wants to show Terrence around"

Travis said, "I will."

A very special friendship began that day and followed them through grade school, junior high and high school, as well as after graduation. When we heard Travis had been killed, we were all so sad, especially Terrence.

He had lost a dear friend and friends were very important to Terrence. We had some long discussions on death and life after death; each of us shared our opinions but more importantly, our beliefs. We came to the agreement that God works in ways we didn't know or understand, realizing that is how it was supposed to be. We are not God, but we by faith completely trust and know He is control.

Terrence was a great writer, and it came easy for him to write his feelings, as well as express himself. We have found many random writings, beliefs, and letters that Terrence wrote over the years around our house, as well as on our computer. The following is one such writing that I found on the computer.

It is unbelievable to me, the faith, insight and hope Terrence had in his "forever" home. There was this core solidness to his belief in his living that I did not know fully, but it is so clear to me as I continue this "moment by moment" journey without him.

Written by Terrence Glenn Skinner
October 24, 2004

One of the most common and challenging questions we Christians face is, "Why do we face such trials and tribulations in our lives?" I do not have or claim to know the answers why we face such trials in our everyday lives, but I do know that there is a loving God in Heaven who is so much bigger than myself and he has a definite plan for my life and yours as well, and his plans are to prosper, not harm us. As we walk through our lives, we will continually run into difficulties that may or may not create a threat to our faith in the Lord, such as sickness, the death of a loved one, a rebellious child, or a job that you hate.

These trials we face daily, which test us as fire refines, lead us to being a more settled, stable Christian in character; and as we continue to seek the Lord during those difficult times, perseverance will be able to finish its work of developing us into strong unshakeable believers. I Peter 1:7 states, "These trials are only to test your faith, to show that it is strong and pure. It is being tested as fire tests and purifies gold, and your faith is far more precious to

God than mere gold. So if your faith remains strong after being tried by fiery trials, it will bring you much praise and glory and honor on the day when Jesus Christ is revealed to the whole world." (New Living Translation Bible). James 1:2-3 also states that "Dear brothers and sisters, whenever trouble comes your way, let it be an opportunity for joy. For when your faith is tested, your endurance has a chance to grow." (New Living Translation Bible)

This doesn't mean we won't have doubt because we are humans and at times we will. But what we're proving is that our hope and trust in Him, Jesus. When this happens, He will reveal His strength, comfort, grace, and unchanging love, and we develop perseverance. With this perseverance we no longer have to rely on things of the world such as drugs, alcohol, or suicide to deal with our trials, but we can turn to the Lord Jesus who takes a bad situation and use it to show us His grace and love.

When we face trials we need to be sure that we're praying and seeking God for his wisdom in making the right decisions.

I have faced many trials in my life, and will continue to do so until the day I get to be with Jesus in Eternity. What I've tried to show you in the above paragraphs is that there is something much bigger going on than what we are seeing right in front of us. God isn't picking on you; He has an awesome plan for your life. I can't say I always agree with or understand His plan, but I hold onto the fact that someday all will be revealed to me, and all will finally make sense when I am called to be with Him in Eternity."

It is true. We do "get to go," but it is a choice we all have the privilege of making. There are many theories, beliefs, opinions and religions that have their own belief on life after death, as well as many who believe there is no afterlife.

I can only speak what I believe and know as truth that I base my life on and live by. I believe every one of us has a spirit that was designed specifically for each one of us; no two are alike. We were each created with a unique and "you" only DNA by God, the only one, true raised from the grave deity.

"FOR GOD SO LOVED THE WORLD THAT HE GAVE HIS ONE AND ONLY SON, THAT WHOEVER BELIEVES IN HIM SHALL NOT PERISH BUT HAVE ETERNAL LIFE." JOHN 3:16

The Resurrection

"AFTER THE SABBATH, AT DAWN ON THE FIRST DAY OF THE WEEK, MARY MAGDALENE AND THE OTHER MARY WENT TO LOOK AT THE TOMB. THERE WAS A VIOLENT EARTHQUAKE, FOR AN ANGEL OF THE LORD CAME down from Heaven, and going to the tomb rolled back the stone and sat on it. His appearance was like lightning, and his clothes were white as snow. The guards were so afraid of him that they shook and became like dead men.

The angel said to the women, "Do not be afraid, for I know that you are looking for Jesus, who was crucified. He is not here; he has risen, just as he said. Come and see the place where he lay. Then go quickly and tell his disciples: "He has risen from the dead and is going ahead of you into Galilee. There you will see him. 'Now I have told you.'"

So the women hurried away from the tomb, afraid yet filled with joy, and ran to tell his disciples. Suddenly Jesus met them, "Greetings," he said. They came to him, clasped his feet and worshipped him. Then Jesus said to them, "Do not be afraid. Go and tell my brothers to go to Galilee; there they will see me." Matthew 28:1-10 (NIV)

Through my life I have heard people speak of "near death" experiences, I have seen the documentaries on such and heard countless stories on "near death." I can say I know without a doubt that Heaven is real, and we do "get to go."

I want to also share that as real as Heaven is, so is

hell. I remember when I was in grade school, being in a room of adults who spoke of a man who was dying. They were recounting how he was frantically tossing and sweating profusely, crying out, "No, no, it's so hot." Now, he had been injured, and if I am recalling correctly, he was very much in a life and death fight for his life.

Little did he know that I am certain he was in a life and death fight for his soul. I believe he saw and felt "hell," literally. As there is a Heaven we can choose to be a part of, there is a hell we choose by not surrendering our life to God.

I do not write this to scare anyone or plant fear, but to simply say, "This society and world we live in promotes that if we're just kind enough; if we do enough "good" things, if we do enough charitable things, if we are a "good" person, that is sufficient to see God. I am sorry to say, that is not the case."

"FEAR THE LORD YOUR GOD, SERVE HIM ONLY AND TAKE YOUR OATHS IN HIS NAME. DO NOT FOLLOW OTHER GODS, THE GODS OF THE PEOPLES AMONG YOU." DEUTERONOMY 6:13-14 (NIV)

I know without a doubt when Terrence took his last earthly breath, he instantly began breathing celestial air. He became a part of a world and afterlife that we who love the Lord, are going to be a part of.

I clearly could feel and see the presence of God

that rested on Terrence in his Critical Care room after he went to be with Jesus. A peace rested on him; a blanket of love was upon him, literally. I don't think anyone can understand fully the "peace that passes all understanding" like I did when entering that hospital room.

"TRUST IN THE LORD WITH ALL YOUR HEART AND LEAN NOT ON YOUR OWN UNDERSTANDING." PROVERBS 3:5 (NIV)

"DO YOU NOT KNOW? HAVE YOU NOT HEARD? THE LORD IS THE EVERLASTING GOD, THE CREATOR OF THE ENDS OF THE EARTH. HE WILL NOT GROW TIRED OR WEARY, AND HIS UNDERSTANDING NO ONE CAN FATHOM." ISAIAH 40:28 (NIV)

There are days that my sadness and loss is so deep that only the promise of Heaven is what gets me through those moments. If it were not for the hope I have in Heaven because of God's immeasurable love for me, I don't know what I would do some days. I have thought it more times than I can number regarding the death of loved ones and the inconsolable grief there would be in not knowing that Terrence rests safely and forever "in the arms of love."

I know many parents personally who have lost sons, and I continue to pray for their comfort, peace and joy that can come only from the Lord. The peace that rests on the countenance of a parent who can confidently know their child is safely home, there is no greater gift that I know of.

An even greater privilege we are given as parents, other than being trusted to raise the precious ones God allows us to have, is to guide them in the truth of Jesus.

I know from experience there comes the time when they are old enough to be on their own or "outside" of your covering as a parent, but that never meant that I didn't stop crying out for my children. I join many parents who continue to spend hours praying for the children, their spouses, and children. What an honor to spend time with the Father, letting our "heart's desires" be known and accept that we have done what we are asked to do.

The hard part comes in letting go of those precious "prayers, pleas, and requests," and let God do what He is best at, His job. So many times I have boldly gone into the throne room crying, asking and even laying down my requests, and I am even better at snatching them up quickly and running out. You see, I think I can take care of the situation better than God, and don't always trust Him to do what he has told me over and over that He will do.

"Do not be anxious about anything, but in everything, by prayer and petition, with thanksgiving, present your request to God."
Philippians 4:5 (NIV)

I have learned that I am still learning the part about "but in everything, by prayer and petition." There are the things of this life that seem less important than others, and I can take care of them! Who am I kidding? There is not one thing that I can do or gain in this life that is not a direct plan or blessing from God.

I sat in the Critical Care waiting room and prayed, "Your will, Father." I knew what that meant as I prayed it, but little did I know what walking out that prayer would mean over the days, weeks, months and years that have followed. I don't regret that prayer for one minute. I know who is in control and the Lord was very much on his throne that December morning. I knew "His will" was going to be fulfilled; I just didn't know what that meant.

My faith, my love for the Lord, my hope in Heaven, and everything that I know is true of His word confirms that Terrence is with the Lord and there is not one doubt in my mind or humanness that doesn't know, "I get to go, too."

Chapter 8
Life Happens

"CONSIDER IT PURE JOY, MY BROTHERS, WHENEVER YOU FACE TRIALS OF MANY KINDS, BECAUSE YOU KNOW THAT THE TESTING OF YOUR FAITH DEVELOPS PERSEVERANCE. PERSEVERANCE MUST FINISH ITS WORK SO THAT YOU MAY BE MATURE AND COMPLETE, NOT LACKING ANYTHING." JAMES 1:2-4 (NIV)

So much has happened and so much life has transpired since Terrence went to Jesus. When we were so fresh in the grief, those early weeks and months we never once thought about "future" things in any long-term measure. It was a good day if I made it through it, and shut the door behind me when I got home.

As I stated in one of the earlier chapters, Lee and I both went back to work within a week of Terrence's death. For me, it was a choice to go back that soon. I was given unconditional love and grace at my job.

Lee's job was quite the opposite; every employer is not the same, and we just kept moving day to day, one foot in front of the other. In hindsight, I am very thankful we went back to work, kept up the illusion of our attempt at "normal" and continued in the routine as best we could.

The daily "stuff" is what helped me make it through in the earthly realm; in the eternal realm, it was the complete love, comfort and hope that I had in Jesus. I cannot imagine how hopeless mankind would be if not for the Love of a Father who would give His only Son.

"THE LORD IS GOOD TO THOSE WHOSE HOPE IS IN HIM, TO THE ONE WHO SEEKS HIM." LAMENTATIONS 3:25

I pray that I am a living testimony to the goodness of God; whom I have sought with wailing and lamenting. My hope is steadfast in his promises and love that I have been shown, received and know is yet to be revealed to me in all its fullness.

The year after Terrence died, October of 2009, I was laid off from the job I had been at for 21 years. I wasn't completely surprised by 'being let go,' but I did feel betrayed, used up, and an easy fix to their "bottom line." I understand business, and I know there were and are hard decisions to be made as an employer. Every day people are facing far greater perils and financial devastation than I will know or be asked to face. But at that time of being laid off, I wasn't completely embracing that part of my journey! I once again was faced with the choice to walk out by faith in all of the truths I knew and to stand firm in "whose" I was, not "who" was signing my checks.

Move ahead in time about 1-1/2 years to spring of 2011. I received a call from a new owner of that business from which I had been laid off. I am back at work there. God is a good. I am so glad I see and know only that which I am to see and know.

There was much I learned in that timeframe of being laid off, and I am very thankful for each part and piece of that season. I am extremely thankful to be back in an industry I enjoy. The extra blessings are the customers who I get to see again, working with new ownership and seeing God's faithfulness to the business.

Terrence's 8th Grade Promotion.

We are experiencing blessings, and I believe that is because there is Godly blessing. We are experiencing blessings and I believe that is because there is Godly leading and the desires are for Kingdom purposes not worldly.

Lee was in an accident two days before Valentine's Day in 2010. He was going to work. He was 1-1/2 blocks from home turning onto a major highway that goes through Halsey. As he turned onto the road, a pickup truck hit him in his driver's side door, crushing the door, spinning him in the opposite direction he was going. He was taken by ambulance to the local hospital, to the same ER we had been in 14 months earlier with Terrence. It was quite overwhelming and very "heavy" while we waited. They did x-rays. He fractured three or four ribs, was bruised and shaken up pretty badly. I remember when I finally got in to see Lee, how he just looked sad. He was physically hurt, but his heart was hurting, too.

It was quite surreal, but we made it out of there, praise God. I went and got the car, and they brought Lee to me in a wheelchair. I helped him into the car. We just sat there under the covering of the ER area, neither of us saying anything, feeling so many emotions and not sure what to do with it all. I said to Lee, "Praise God you are coming home with me, Honey." He smiled through the tears.

He was off work for four to six weeks, which in itself turned out to be quite a challenging time, but God was faithful to us once again.

The above "life" stuff I mention only to show that things happen; we make choices in those times of testing, and we have to decide what we're going to do. We all have choices; every day there are choices to be made. Lee and I have hopefully made Godly choices that have brought blessing to us and those around us. That is our desire.

Terrence's Senior Graduation 1998.

"BLESSED IS THE MAN WHO PERSEVERES UNDER TRIAL, BECAUSE WHEN HE HAS STOOD THE TEST HE WILL RECEIVE THE CROWN OF LIFE THAT GOD HAS PROMISED TO THOSE WHO LOVE HIM." JAMES 1:12

Along this "life' journey we are on, my mom went to Jesus July 3, 2011.

On January of 2011, Mom had a heart episode and

ended up in a Heart and Vascular unit of a local hospital. Her cardiologist gave the timeframe of six months for us to have Mom. I remember sitting in the waiting area of Mom's wing; the doctor and all of us kids gathered to listen to his expert opinion and to have us all consider our options, to make decisions on medical measures we would want used on Mom.

My mom had deteriorating health for years. She lived in her own place, but had caregivers come in Monday through Saturday during the days. After mom came home from the hospital in January, her children took turns at nights and on weekends being with her. For me personally, this was a time to just hang out with Mom. I came to love the Hallmark Channel and the Gospel Channel Mom got. I shared at her funeral in South Dakota (where she was laid to rest next to Dad) that I still see her feet and toes a tapping to the "Gaither Gospel Hour" that we watched on weekends.

It was a blessing to be one of Mom's caregivers. I learned so much about God's grace and unconditional love during those months with Mom. I remember thinking what a blessing it was that we were getting to take care of Mom, and what we were doing for her, when in reality it was Mom who showed me so much more through that time.

I got to see perseverance like had never seen it before. I saw the calm and peace of Jesus that rested on Mom. I miss her, but also know as we are into the eighth year without Terrence that we serve an amazing, loving and wise God.

After Mom died, I shared with my family that we would feel like orphans, but His Word says otherwise.

"I WILL NOT LEAVE YOU AS ORPHANS; I WILL COME TO YOU." JOHN 14:18 (NIV)

God has not left me as an orphan. He has come to me as He did even before Mom died, and as He continues to come and rest upon and with me, always.

The view from Terrence's grave.
I find great peace in this pastoral setting.

Chapter 9
No Regrets

"FOR I KNOW THE PLANS I HAVE FOR YOU," DECLARES THE LORD," PLANS TO PROSPER YOU AND NOT TO HARM YOU, PLANS TO GIVE YOU HOPE AND A FUTURE."
JEREMIAH 29:11 (NIV)

God did not say it would be a perfect journey, but he did promise a perfect destination.

As time has passed (years, actually), I am realizing that there is life after death; especially for me as a mother, after losing a son. I knew immediately after Terrence went home to be with Jesus that my life, and life around me would continue, but I didn't have any idea how sad and lost I would be in that process.

The planning and details that need immediate attention after the passing of a loved one plunge you into days that are a blur. You make all the critical, immediate decisions; you meet at the funeral home and walk through a process that guts you wide open while you continue to breathe.

Then, you stand at an open grave with your loved one hovering above that cold, black, open hole on a pulley system that will be lowering them into the ground, to be covered with dirt. Nothing prepares you for what you have to do and what you have to walk through when your child dies, or for that matter when anyone you love and would give your own life for dies.

What a comfort I have, even in my tremendous numb and broken state in knowing there was and is a God in Heaven who loved me so much that Terrence is now with Him. What a peace to never have doubted since Terrence's death where he is right now. He is safely in the arms of love, surrounded by more light, peace and wholeness than he has ever known. Alive and whole, what a promise from God that is mine, to know this! And, we will meet again in Heaven.

"SEE THAT WHAT YOU HAVE HEARD FROM THE BEGINNING REMAINS IN YOU. IF IT DOES, YOU ALSO WILL REMAIN IN THE SON AND IN THE FATHER. AND THIS IS WHAT HE PROMISED US—EVEN ETERNAL LIFE."
I JOHN 2: 24-25 (NIV)

There are the memories that flood you at first. Then with the years, they come and go with their sadness and intensity somewhat subdued. There are the days that you don't know if you can breathe.

You wonder, "Did all this really happen," and "Is he really gone?" Your life is so adjusted, altered, that it is so hard to believe this is "really" how it is going to be until Jesus calls you home. Numerous times I have asked Lee, "If this is my life for years to come, I don't want to do it."

Then, I can so clearly hear my Terrence saying, "Come on, Moms, don't be like that; you can do this." And, I move forward into the next minutes and hours knowing that the dearest soul I ever knew this side of Heaven is in the throne room, worshipping and bowing before God almighty.

Lee has asked me over the years, "If we got a 'do-over' would you?" My answer is just about always the same, "Why would I want Terrence to leave Heaven to come back here? If everything was to turn out just as it is now, no way."

I am amazed what my Heavenly Father knows about me—that this life I have is exactly where I am to be and what I am to be doing for "this" time. I can hardly wait to see what He knows and knew long before I was even born.

Some days the clarity I have on "this" life and "eternity" is overwhelming and then there are the days! I know that if I have figured it out—that's really not what is important. What's important is "Whose" I am. I was chosen for this journey, every tear and every smile, every triumph and heartache, it is all mine sent from the hands and heart of God.

Terrence had heartache, made mistakes, experienced failures, and he was as human as any person could be. He also made choices in his life that led him straight to the feet of a mighty God sitting on a throne who stood, embraced my Terrence, and said, "Well done."

That is the comfort that I have, the peace that floods my heart when the tears flood my eyes.

There were things, situations, and choices I am sure Terrence would have liked to have had the chance to mend and change. We all choose outside of God's "will" but there is such hope in knowing the immeasurable love that allowed His son to die for our sins past, present, and future. Thank you, Jesus.

Walking through the death of a child has shown

me so much about the love of God, how Mary felt, and the amazing God we serve. I often see Mary running along the crowd, ducking and moving in and out of the people to get a glimpse of that sweet boy she had birthed. She witnessed the hatred, the beating, and the betrayal that her Son endured. I can relate from a mother's heart to Mary. Yet there was so much more her son endured, so mine could spend forever with our Heavenly Father. Thank you, Mary.

I was blessed with the time to tell Terrence "no regrets" in the hospital before he was taken. I loved that kid more than life itself and had told him how much I loved him. Lee and I let our kids know we loved and love them. God was so gracious in giving us two boys that were kind, considerate and all ours.

As a family, we had so much love, that I find myself feeling guilty and wondering if I loved too much, too hard, too fully.

Then the spirit of God tells me, "You loved exactly as I created you to love, deeply, passionately and fully."

"THEY MUST KEEP HOLD OF THE DEEP TRUTHS OF THE FAITH WITH A CLEAR CONSCIENCE." I TIMOTHY KEEP HOLD OF THE DEEP TRUTHS OF THE FAITH WITH A CLEAR CONSCIENCE." I TIMOTHY 3:9

It was not a quick, instantaneous or even a completed "word" for us, but it is and has been a work and "word" in process. I have clung to the deep truths of my faith; pretty sure not always with a clear conscience, but a conscience of conviction in the immeasurable, never-ending, always present love of Jesus.

December 26, 2012

Today marks four years since we had Terrence's funeral, laying his body to rest. I find myself surrounded by Terrence's presence and covered by a love that passes all human understanding. Many days, "Forever" is an unattainable timeframe, and then there is today when it seems so close, almost tangible. I feel and have come to know Kingdom on so many levels since that cold, awful, gut wrenching day four years ago.

I know I serve a God who is superior to any other gods, who loves me beyond my understanding or ability to accept. Terrence is alive today, more than any time in his life. He is with my mom, dad, brothers, and so many loved ones who wait for me. I am stronger than I ever knew possible in my "truths and my faith" than any time in my life.

I miss Terrence with every breath I take, but I can say "no regrets" today as I did so many days ago. I know Terrence doesn't miss me and that's OK. I even catch myself smiling sometimes when I'm telling him how much I miss him. I can see that sweet face with that grin of his saying, "Love you too, Moms, and can hardly wait to see you." My family is good. We are seeing God in our life and know He is at work, healing, holding, restoring, and redeeming.

As Christmas neared again this year, and we all prepared for another "marker" in our life (another year without Terrence), I felt a hope and peace resting on me. Christmas morning, I was up early and could so clearly see Terrence gazing into the face of God, and it brought me such comfort. As I knew four years ago, I knew this Christmas morning 2012 that Terrence was with "Christmas." Gathered with the Saints of old, praising, and worshipping like it was just another day, (which I guess for so many I love who are with Jesus, was another "forever" day.)

What an incredible thought, that every day in Heaven is Christmas. Not as we know it here with the commercialism, trimmings, and trappings, but being with our Heavenly Father and a part of Kingdom.

"DAY AND NIGHT THEY NEVER STOP SAYING: "HOLY, HOLY, HOLY IS THE LORD GOD ALMIGHTY, WHO WAS, AND IS AND IS TO COME." REVELATION 4:8

My happiest thoughts of eternity are hearing, "Well done, good and faithful servant," and being a part of the hosts gathered, worshipping and praising the risen, living God. Oh, what a day that will be.

I have tried to be more aware of the green in the trees and grass, the sun that only peeks out now and then through our Oregon winters, the laughter of kids down the street, the barking of the dogs in the distance.

There are countless blessings in our everyday life that are easy to get used to and take for granted. When things are good, we don't seem to have that desperation or need for God. But when things turn bad, situations and circumstances out of our control, we find ourselves crying out with desperation that we never knew existed.

"GIVE THANKS IN ALL CIRCUMSTANCES, FOR THIS IS GOD'S WILL FOR YOU IN CHRIST JESUS." I THESSALONIANS 5:8 (NIV)

The interesting part of the above verse that has become clearer to me is where it says, "…this is God's will for you in Christ Jesus." I knew the importance of giving thanks in all circumstances, but never really understood or found the need to understand the "why" of the verse. Of course, God's will for me in Christ Jesus is to give thanks in all circumstances!

I didn't see this verse that way until I walked through the "valley of death" and grief like I never knew was possible. The exciting encouragement is God knows me so well, and every overly human part of me, but in spite of all of it, He loves me unconditionally.

"ETERNITY IS NOT SOMETHING THAT BEGINS AFTER YOU ARE DEAD. IT IS GOING ON ALL THE TIME. WE ARE IN IT NOW."

Charlotte Perkins

I forget that every day I have "now" is eternity happening right around and in me. God is eternal, ever present, always available, never-ending, unconditionally loving, and He loves me.

I have come to realize the constant need for "truth" in my life, and the only "truth" that has sustained and held me through my darkest hours, has been the Bible. I love reading from the New International Bible (NIV). The Bible I have is the one Lee gave to me.

I have an amazing husband who is a man of God and loves me and walks this life with me as my best friend. He loves the Lord. He loves me. He loves our sons and people in general. It is a true gift to have a "constant" in my life who will always be loving God, me and others. We live in a world so consumed with "self" and all of the lies that go with self-absorption, so it is comforting to not worry of such folly.

My prayer for you, the reader, is to live your life with "no regrets." Embrace this life we are all a very purposed part of. Ask for forgiveness often, give love freely and expect nothing in return. Encourage others, listen wholeheartedly, hug often, smile, laugh, share your journey. Show random acts of kindness. Live "now." Don't long for yesterday or look only for tomorrow, but live for the present moment and embrace every moment and be present.

I have learned to live "moment by moment" in ways I never thought I could or would, nor wanted to, but it is possible. You will find strength, courage, grace, mercy, love and hope in places and people you will be amazed at, when you didn't even know how desperately you needed them.

Sing, O son of Zion
Shout, O child of mine
Rejoice with all your heart and soul and mind
Sing, O daughter of Zion
Cry out, O child of mine
And dance with all the strength that you can find
For you are finally home

Every tear you cried dried in the palm of my hand
Every lonely hour was by my side
Every loved one lost, every river crossed
Every moment, every hour was pointing to this day
I've been longing for this day

Chapter 10
More than Survivors

"Indeed he was sick almost unto death; but God had mercy on him, and not only on him, but on me also, lest I should have sorrow upon sorrow." Philippians 2:27 (NKJV)

"Who, by the power that enables him to bring everything under his control, will transform our lowly bodies so that they will be like his glorious body." Philippians 3:21 (NIV)

"Faith is daring the soul to go beyond what the eyes can see."

Zig Ziglar

Grief is a natural response to loss. It is the emotional suffering. These two sentences put into words, is what we have walked through the last 8 years. There is so much more to death, loss, grief, whatever word you want to use, that it is impossible to find the correct "phraseology" to adequately express the darkest, saddest place we have had to walk out. Take heart, there is such hope we have in this journey, filled with every tear, heartache, and beat of our heart that longs for Terrence.

Grieving with hope, still hurts.

We have had (and continue to have) a hope that can't be quantified or verbalized as completely as we would like. We do hope our lives show the unbelievable anchor that is ours, through Jesus and the promises of Forever.

We don't live looking to the future and just longing to see Terrence; we are called, positioned, and placed "for such a time as this." Lee and I know without one single doubt or hesitation; we will see Terrence again. But until then, there is a purpose and plan the Father has for our lives, which we try to walk in the fullness of every day.

"FOR I KNOW THE PLANS I HAVE FOR YOU," DECLARES THE LORD, "PLANS TO PROSPER YOU AND NOT TO HARM YOU, PLANS TO GIVE YOU HOPE AND A FUTURE." JEREMIAH 29:11 (NIV)

This scripture is my favorite, and I believe it with everything within me; that God's plan for me is to prosper me and to give me a hope and a future. We have been walking in all of those promises and so much more that I don't feel like I deserve, but that is the God we have chosen; the one who lavishes his love, provision, promises and hope on us daily, hourly, and sometimes "moment by moment."

I find it funny to write, "the God we have chosen" when the reality is, HE is the one who has chosen us. He has prepared a table, a banquet is waiting, a mansion is built and a deck is just waiting for me to sit on with Terrence. What I have seen and know of Heaven, it will be as though we have never been apart, picking up right where we left off. For me, in the fleshly form, this side of Heaven, it feels so far off and so long to wait but rest assured in the Father's timeframe, it is a breath and a moment.

Lee and I walk with a futuristic hope and a realistic daily life. Sometimes the "realistic" life is a little tough and some days unbearable, but we do our best to love deeply, give freely and live with abandon. We have had and continue to have, such opportunities to share Terrence's story, his life, his belief and our hope. Our desire is to give honor to God in all that we do, honor Terrence's life and memory and encourage parents, that there is Hope when you bury a piece of you.

"I ALONE CANNOT CHANGE THE WORLD, BUT I CAN CAST A STONE ACROSS THE WATERS TO CREATE MANY RIPPLES."

Mother Teresa

"Divine Appointments" is what my father-in-law calls those exchanges/meetings/coincidences that happen when you are the person for the "moment" in someone else's journey.

We have an opportunity daily to make a difference in this world. We aren't called to be everything for everybody; I believe we are called to be something for somebody. Some days that is a big "something" we are asked to be or do and other days it is the smallest thing that may change a person's day, even your own perspective. I always think of the saying, "Give away a smile, it costs you nothing."

I am caught off guard at times by the simplest things I do every day, that are the very things God uses to impact my little corner of Kingdom or someone else's. I love wandering through the grocery store, doing my shopping and watching people as I go; minding my own business, yet being aware of the opportunity to have a "Divine Appointment."

Lee and I both work full-time jobs. (Well, I just went down to four days a week September of 2016 to watch my granddaughter, Raegan, one day a week.) Nonetheless, we are in the marketplace daily, where we both have had the blessing of those who know us, check in to see how we are doing.

Lee works in our local little town, where he is known at his job and blessed there often by the customers who have come to know, love and appreciate the man he is. We have been blessed by so many with things such as smoked chicken, prime rib, produce, cookies, cakes, pie, Christmas goodies and the list goes on.

I choose to believe that it's "whose" we are not "who" we are.

Our desire has always been to be in relationship not religious. Lee has served on the City Council here in our hometown, and I believe he has done a good job. He is a quiet man, but an amazing listener. He may be a man of few words, but he is a thinker and when he does speak, it is well thought out. (Maybe not what is popular or predicted, but intentional and thoughtful.) That is not always the best "viewpoint" to have in this day and age, but it is "whose" he is. He is a good man and God's man, who I call my husband, with whom I celebrated 38 years of marriage November of 2016.

I have the opportunity and freedom at my work to be "me." God has allowed me to share Terrence's story more than I can count (with most customers in tears) as I proclaim the goodness of God, the thankful mother's heart I have for Terrence dying quickly and not suffering, and the tremendous HOPE we have. Along the way, I have come to be friends, not just an employee, of an establishment that they frequent.

That is the bonus and the blessing I am truly thankful for, as well as the flexibility and friendship with my boss and co-workers.

I have come across parents who have lost a child also, and I've been able to share in their hope and their story. I feel privileged to have those "moment to moment" windows of time with fellow Pilgrims. We each have a "story," and we need each other and the opportunities to tell that story and be heard.

It is not easy being the parent of a "deceased" child. There is an invisible label that we parents wear when we have lost a child; it is awkward and uncomfortable. Those first contacts that are made after the funeral, are rough at best. People have good intentions, wanting to be normal, but it doesn't come easy or very naturally. There is the struggle for conversation, even eye contact is hesitant and calculated. The comfort is, it does get easier. Time passes, we get to choose what we are going to do "moment to moment" as we press forward, adapting to our "new normal."

I have had numerous "gifts/signs" that reassure me Terrence is fine, giving me the hope and the promise I will see him again. Sometime after Terrence was gone, Lyndsay came to visit and was telling me of their morning commutes to their jobs, which they traveled together. She was sharing how she would drive in the mornings and Terrence would turn on a dome light and read a devotional.

I of course was blessed to know that was important to Terrence. Since Terrence's passing, there have been numerous times when I will get into my car(s) and there will be a dome light on. And, on several occasions, both dome lights are on!

Lee goes to work very early when it is still pitch dark. One of the most recent dome light moments happened in the morning when I went to go to work. It was still very dark and both dome lights were on in my car. When Lee left at 4:55 AM, there were no lights on in my car. My car doors were locked and the lights were on, which I know was a "sign" that Terrence is in eternal "light" and is doing just fine.

Terrence would spend hours, sitting with us on the decks sharing, loving and laughing. The morning we ran home to get Lee's medicine and go back to the hospital for what would be only mere hours before Terrence would be gone, there was an obvious "absence" in "his" chair on the deck.

As we pulled under the carport, I got out and just stood there, sensing a "shift" and heaviness that was tangible surrounding us, the deck, and our home. I knew we needed to hurry so we could get back to the hospital, but it almost seemed as though time stood still. As I entered the house, I remember going from room to room, keenly aware something was missing, different and shifting.

Little did I know, it wouldn't be until later that morning that those moments in our home, the clarity and finality would be sealed in Eternity. The "shift" I was feeling, I am certain was what I have been a part of on numerous other occasions, death. God is such a gentlemen and loves me so much, there are more times than I can recount, I am sure, where I have had the privilege and honor of being "prepared."

I know this concept may be difficult to process, especially when we had to walk away from a hospital and leave the body of our son, whom we adored. But that is the best I can explain that portion of our journey. It in no way was easy, without tremendous heartache, lamenting, sorrow and beyond our human comprehension, but it was possible with the leading of the "Spirit" sent to us fully and boldly from the Throne. A personal savior given, so my son lives eternally and we will see him again.

There was a supernatural presence that carried and maintained Lee and me in those early hours and days. We knew there were people waiting for us to leave the hospital and get to our house. It was unreal that we walked down that hall from Critical Care and were leaving Terrence there to be picked up for "transport" to the funeral home. I was walking through the worst nightmare ever, with my eyes wide open and my heart shattered. There is absolutely nothing that prepares you for intense reality and separation that happens when you lose your loved one.

Lee and I like hummingbirds; we are mesmerized by the speed and agility they have. At some of our saddest, hardest days, there will be a hummingbird that seems to find us sitting on the deck. It will hover for a while, allowing us to see it and then fly off. One of the times I was outside, a hummingbird fluttered up to the edge of the deck, saw me, hovered toward me, remaining suspended, as I was able to just look at it. I believe it was another "sign" that Terrence was just fine.

"Grief is just love with no place to go."

I saw this posted on my cousin's Facebook page; the unlikely irony is, she lost a child also, her daughter. I know I have mentioned in a previous chapter that, "If you love deeply, you hurt deeply." There are so many commonalities I see now, that I did not see before, in the grieving community. Isn't that a lovely word, grieving community, but that is what we are an official member of, not from just Terrence dying but so many other loved ones we've said goodbye to. There has not been, nor do I ever remember, the level of grief that we have experienced, like we have in losing Terrence. The promise in where we are present day, is that we are choosing life and love, standing as victorious conquerors. We are so much more than just surviving our loss, we are daily choosing to wake, walk, work and welcome whatever is ours to give or receive for that day.

I was listening to a webcast from a dad who lost his daughter on December 20th, five years after Terrence died. His daughter was only five years old! He was talking about feeling "gutted" as he and his family continued to work their way through their loss. I shared with a friend and numerous other times, how I felt like Darth Vader took his light saber, cut me right down the middle, exposing all of my brokenness and grief, for every one to see.

I have come to live through, conquer and be put back together piece by piece; creating my "new normal." God in all of his mercy and love, met me right where I was and went to work. When sleep doesn't come, He is right there. When I can't take another step, He takes my hand and leads me, even carries me at times. When the sadness overwhelms me like a wave pulling me under, with crying that I don't think will end, He lets me crawl up in his lap and rest until I can move on. I am not who I was when Terrence died, and I am not who I was last year, and I will be a different person in the years to come.

There are times I get scared and panic trying to remember Terrence's voice. There is a video I have of

Terrence goofing around and laughing, the summer before he died, which I am so thankful for. I miss his laughter, and I miss his smile. He gave the best hugs and had the most amazing sense of humor. The one thing I am certain of, is the hope I have of Forever, the promises of Kingdom and of seeing Terrence again. It won't be as I knew Terrence on Earth, but nonetheless it will be Terrence. I won't shed another tear, spend another sleepless night or wish I could see him, I will be with him, that is the hope I cling to "moment to moment."

I have taken one day a week off from my work, to help take care of our granddaughter, Raegan; I love that little girl beyond measure. I play with her on the floor, loving every minute. I rock her, watch her breathe, see her eyes flutter, see her stretch. She is such a trusting little girl, relies on someone to feed her, to change her diaper, to burp her, to bathe her, to teach her. I am learning so much about Kingdom principles as I watch Raegan. I have come to a deeper understanding of the scripture that says,

"TRULY I TELL YOU, ANYONE WHO WILL NOT RECEIVE THE KINGDOM OF GOD LIKE A LITTLE CHILD WILL NEVER ENTER IT." MARK 10:15 NIV

We are healing, moving, embracing loving and see the fullness in every day we are given. Some days are easier than others but we are doing it, "moment to moment."

My desire is that you have found hope, love and joy in these pages, that can and will sustain you in the darkest places you may have to face. We are never alone and there is a hope and sustainer, that will hold you when the storms of this life rage and beat at your very core. I pray with each chapter you read, you got to know Terrence and the anchor he had in his life, the hope that holds Lee and me, strengthening our faith with each year that we live without Terrence. As well as, the joy that we have always known, even when we faced the hardest time in our life.

I leave you with the following scripture, which has been the promise and hope that continues to build our Faith, daily and "moment to moment."

"FOR I KNOW THE PLANS I HAVE FOR YOU," DECLARES THE LORD, "PLANS TO PROSPER YOU AND NOT TO HARM YOU, PLANS TO GIVE YOU HOPE AND A FUTURE."

JEREMIAH 29:11 (NIV)

About the Author

Sharlene Campbell-Skinner's story began in the farm country of Central South Dakota. She is the

middle child of seven (three sisters and three brothers). Two of her brothers are with her son, Terrence, in "Forever," as well as both of her parents.

Attending grade school and high school in the same rural area, she married a farm boy, Lee Allen Skinner, and the two of them began their story together in the fall of 1978.

They have made many lifelong relationships throughout the years, counting their greatest achievements as: their choice to have God as their personal Savior, their marriage, and their two sons.

An added joy and light of Sharlene's life, is her granddaughter, Raegan Marie Skinner who was born March 2, 2016. As she enters a new "phase" of her life, she continues to put Faith, Family and Forever first and foremost in her life and choices.

If you would like to know more about Sharlene, her faith and her story (or you would like to obtain more books) contact her at:

Sharlene Campbell-Skinner
PO Box 6
Halsey, OR 97348

Phone: 541-369-2972
Email LSSkinner@rtinet.com.

www.ingramcontent.com/pod-product-compliance
Lightning Source LLC
LaVergne TN
LVHW020930090426
835512LV00020B/3303